REGENERATION

Edited by Clare Coatman & Guy Shrubsole

with Ben Little and Shiv Malik

Regeneration focuses on the question of intergenerational justice. Defining the world's young people as those born after 1979 – a hugely symbolic moment in the history of globalisation – it reflects on the massive growth in generational protest across the globe thirty years later. At its heart is an analysis of politics through the prism of generation.

The incapacity of the major political parties in Britain to think beyond their short-term electoral interests is, by definition, particularly harmful for those at the beginning of their lives. It has led to a failure to act on climate change, savage cutbacks in education and training, an acute shortage of housing, big cuts in youth services, and, for many, the prospect of an old age without pensions. Things have deteriorated to the point where many young people are finding it impossible to find the wherewithal to settle down and have families – the classic marks of adulthood.

But, as Shiv Malik argues in his preface, a diagnosis of the problem does not absolve the young from taking responsibility for developing solutions. We need more than 'a whinge of epic proportions'. And, as he also points out, the young are well placed to develop alternatives: 'we are the most well-educated, innovative, dynamic and open generation in human history'. This means that this book also has plenty of ideas for changing the future.

Contributors: Patrick Ainley, Guy Aitchison, Christo Albor, Martin Allen, Jamie Audsley, Craig Berry, Guppi Bola, Matthew Cheeseman, Clare Coatman, Chris Coltrane, Ray Filar, David Floyd, George Gabriel, Tim Gee, Richard George, Paolo Gerbaudo, Jeremy Gilbert, Deborah Grayson, Noel Hatch, Tim Holmes, Rina Kuusipalo, Ben Little, Becky Luff, Shiv Malik, Peter McColl, John Miers, Jim O'Connell, Adam Ramsay, Kirsty Schneeberger, Guy Shrubsole, Charlie Young.

Series Editor: Ben Little

Assistant Editor: Shiv Malik

Part of the *Radical Future* series.

ISBN 9781907103490

Cover design: Yoav Segal

Cover photographs: Lindsay Mackenzie, Yoav Segal, Jacob Perlmutter
and www.morguefile.co.uk

Typesetting: e-type

Collection as a whole © Lawrence Wishart 2012

Individual articles © the authors 2012

Published by Lawrence & Wishart
Supported by the Intergenerational Foundation and the
Lipman-Miliband Trust

The Intergenerational Foundation (if.org.uk) is delighted to be involved in the publication of *Regeneration*. Our work in promoting the rights of younger and future generations means that we support new thinking, encourage debate and galvanise action in the hope that younger generations will demand more from our political leaders. We hope the pieces here will challenge you to take action as they have challenged us to do.

Angus Hanton, Co-founder, IF

Contents

Foreword

Where's your shame? You've left us up to our necks in it!

David Bowie, Changes, 1971

Hello, welcome and thank you for picking up or downloading *Regeneration*. I was asked to commend this book to you. That's easy, as it's damn fantastic. But to start I want to try something harder. To try and suggest to you that viewing more of the world through a generational lens, the theme that this book is wrapped around, could change your life and those around you forever. And for the better.

In the simplest sense all change happens generationally – a group of people at a certain time opt to make a difference in some rule, law or governing structure, which sets them apart from those that are older – dead or alive – than themselves.

But this statement is also pretty bland. Given this is always the case, what does the claim add to our understanding of how things are changed? In terms of our comprehension of events, isn't what matters the agency behind the change? For conservative historians, it is hierarchies and the individuals in charge which need to be studied and cross-examined to understand the process of change. For those on the left, materialism and stratospheres of class are at the root of making sense of the great shifts in society. Then there are those who hone in on nation states or bureaucracies or gender or race – all distinct prisms to help us understand how change occurs. But what about generations themselves? What role does time and the groups of people born decades apart – both in years, but also in social attitudes, technological influence and economic development – play in making change happen? And because of increasing life expectancy, in a world where more generations are to be found living cheek by jowl than ever before, aren't generations playing a greater role in the dynamic of change than at any other moment in history?

I remember putting the question to Avner Offer, Chichele professor of economic history at All Souls College, Oxford, in early 2010, whilst co-authoring the book *Jilted Generation: how Britain has bankrupted its youth*. An expert on the effect of time on economics and history, not only did Professor Offer scoff at the book's title, he replied bluntly that there is no such thing as a generational change agent in historical terms.

It seemed a bizarre response even then, as the precursor to this book, *Radical Future*, made its way on to our (digital) shelves in April 2010. It seems an even more bizarre response now, after all the recent generational tumult. Whether the August riots, the student movement of late 2010, the encampments on Tahrir square, the violent unrest in Greece, or the occupations of public spaces around the globe – these are movements that have been primarily characterised by the presence and/or the collective leadership of the world's young people – defined in this book as those born after 1979, a choice date for pinpointing the start of globalisation, but also, coincidentally, the beginning of a demographic mini-boom in most countries, popularly known in the USA as the baby-boom echo.

More than thirty years after being fostered by the environmental movement, intergenerational justice – the main trunk of generational enquiry – is still viewed with suspicion by those on the traditional left. For a start, it apparently holds all the wrong antagonistic qualities when compared to class warfare – why fight the vested interests of your parents when you should be fighting those of the upper classes? Or to put it another way, how does fighting the baby boomers stop the fat cats from making off with society's plunder? Secondly, there ain't much on generational analysis to be found in the writings and traditions of the left, which again is mainly steeped in class. This makes for a harder integration into left politics. Thirdly, those on the right seem to have taken up the mantle of the fiscal discipline deemed necessary if one generation is to be just to another. All the more reason to be suspicious.

More detailed retorts to these issues (and many more) are to be found throughout this stunning collection of essays bound by the theme of re-generation. But here is a broad answer to those who are unsure of what generational analysis has to offer them.

Firstly, the generational lens is a tool for understanding current problems in a new way. For example, how government austerity cuts fall and upon whom is very instructive. It's plain to see that the poorest suffered the most. But it's far more politically pertinent to notice that it was the young who were forced to take most of the burden. Whether it was EMA, student fee rises brought about by the swinging broadside to higher education teaching budgets, the slashing of housing benefits to younger adults (including the highly age-discriminatory raising of the shared-room rate age from 25 to 35), rent caps (which again primarily affect young people), or youth service cuts (and the list goes on); it was younger people (and the poorest amongst those) who were selected to pay for the bailout caused by generations above.

Dig deeper into how budgets and spending have shifted over time, and the trend of cutting from the young seems to be a long-term process, mandated by parties of all stripes. What is revealed is a damaging culture of political short-termism and the flowering of neoliberalism's malign effects – a construct which itself allows for no mechanism for making long-term plans.

In a sense politicians have also grasped at the chance to cut from a generation that knows no better because they have experienced nothing else. It is intergenerational comparisons that remind us that when they were our age, our parents had houses built for them not in the hundreds but in the hundreds of thousands every year; they enjoyed fixed private rents, and many of them grew up in a time when unemployment was astonishingly low.

But if things were once different, they can be different once again.

The generational lens also helps illuminate current political struggles. 2011 saw unions take strike action not seen for decades. For many at the fore of the student movement, this was an unmitigated good. Here, finally, were workers joining with students – the holy alliance of revolutionary politics. Yet when unions ask for better pensions, they ask the government, who in turn have decided to push the cost onto the young as a generation, as opposed to those who can best afford it – which surely includes the young, but also today's working rich, who will now be let off from their full responsibilities.

Intergenerational justice demands we ask whether this is fair, especially when over 90 per cent of young people aren't even saving for a pension and many can't afford to do so. They certainly won't enjoy those private pension payment holidays that those working in the 1990s were allowed to take. Ultimately, young people need to help unions and government – both of whom suffer from a failure of political imagination and will – to find more just solutions to this issue and others like it.

Secondly, generational analysis helps us to see new problems ahead. As is not uncommon with youth across Europe, the United States and North Africa, Britain's youth are now caught in the bind of precarious low paid work and insecure and unaffordable housing. Under these conditions, how will the family unit fare? And if a whole generation becomes dependent on the state or their parents, what becomes of the concept of adulthood? Is it postponed, does it morph, or does it breakdown altogether? And then what of our concepts of work, consumerism, individualism, and our desire for security and notions of freedom?

To take a Marxist bent, as material conditions change, how do the social relations, not of a class of people but of a generation within society, change, adapt and reform? Newly identified problems also mean prospects for new solutions. One of the chapters in this book proposes that we institute the post of Ombudsman for future generations as a solution to the issue of the political short-termism that now blights our generation's lives.

Thirdly, a generational perspective allows us to get to grips with what is happening within a generation of people itself; to turn the intergenerational mirror upon ourselves if you like. The post-79'ers have a set of mores, attitudes and abilities somewhat distinct from those older than them. These need to be recognised in order to better appreciate what solutions and actions will and won't work.

In more ways than one, we are Thatcher's children, so how will we fix the problem of political and economic individualism, when as a generation we are socially individualistic to an astonishing degree? In his chapter, Noel Hatch asks whether we must face further collective suffering before we find a collective voice – to become poorer before we become more powerful.

Finally, generational analysis grounds us in an energetic political constituency. As I see it, intergenerational politics does not call for an attack on the older generation for what they have bequeathed to us. Those who propound the 'blame the boomers' line desperately misunderstand how our generation has had its economic and environmental security eroded, and what lies behind the push for that change. As Tim Gee puts it in his chapter, 'Our antagonism cannot be towards our parents' generation per se, but towards the ideas and decisions of unaccountable elites'.

But even if done correctly, blame is somewhat easy to apportion. Who takes responsibility for clearing up the mess is the bigger and more inspiring political calling. Is it the job of individual leaders, political parties, unions, the apparatus of the nation state, NGOs and the international community, or our generation – the people who in the end must deal with the consequences? I believe responsibility must reside with my generation. Without responsibility for bringing about the cure, the diagnosis alone is just a whinge of epic proportions.

To those who try to stop the changes necessary to correcting our problems, we must reply with the same full-throated retort that Bowie penned for his generation: 'Where is your shame? You've left us up to our neck in it!' Whether it's the pensioner on the parish

council who stands in the way of building social housing because
he doesn't want to see his own property devalued, or the baby-
boomer head of a multinational who says action over climate
change is hindering productivity, the retort should be the same –
where's your shame?

The problems we have inherited from our elders are huge. But
we must remember that we are the most well-educated, innovative,
dynamic and open generation in human history. There is much that
will remake the world in the coming years. It's just one of those
moments in history which we find ourselves living in. I hope that
this book can help illuminate the way.

Shiv Malik, Cofounder Intergenerational Foundation,
8 January 2012

Shiv Malik started his career as a freelance journalist working for
the *New Statesman*. He has gone on to work for *The Sunday Times*,
the *Independent*, and the BBC, amongst others. He has reported
from Afghanistan and Pakistan and now works for *The Guardian* as
an investigative journalist. In 2010 he co-authored *Jilted Generation:
how Britain has bankrupted its youth*. He is also a founder member of
the think tank, the Intergenerational Foundation.

Introduction

Guy Shrubsole & Clare Coatman

> Bliss was it in that dawn to be alive. But to be young was
> very heaven!
>
> William Wordsworth, 1799

We live, as the ancient Chinese curse would have it, in interesting times. A world on the brink of a Great Depression. A right-wing government in Britain determined to impose austerity and the creeping privatisation of public services. Technocrats replacing elected politicians in Greece and Italy, the cradles of democracy. Spiralling inequality and a planet in peril. To be young in these times is seldom bliss: what prospect heaven when a million young people are unemployed and our earthly inheritance is going up in smoke?

When the young poet Wordsworth penned his ecstatic eulogy to youth, the cause of his joy was the hope promised by the French Revolution.[1] To eighteenth-century European societies, hidebound by tradition and labouring under the weight of oppressive monarchies, the demands of the French *sans-culottes* – liberty, equality, fraternity! – promised to remake the world and break utterly with history. And so they did: the French Revolution founded the modern political concepts of left and right, and kick-started faith in progress – that history is an upward ascent; that the world we leave to our children will always be a little better than the world we inherited.

For the majority of our childhood, adolescence and young adulthood, history is primarily something that has been done to us. Our generation – those who were born in the years since 1979 – were still young when swaggering commentators declared 'the end of history', and the final triumph of free-market capitalism over all other possible forms of society.[2] The fall of the Berlin Wall and the collapse of communism wiped away a decrepit set of repressive regimes. But as they crumbled, something else was also eroded: a belief in alternatives to the status quo.

It is not as if the current system has exactly performed well. As we started school, a panoply of greying statesmen gathered at Rio de Janeiro to pledge themselves 'determined to protect the climate system for present and future generations'.[3] Their determination has borne fruit in twenty years of accelerating carbon emissions. We sat our GCSEs whilst world trade talks ground to a halt in Seattle, and took our A-levels as wars for resources were waged in the Middle East. We applied for our first jobs amidst the collapse of Lehman Brothers.[4] History returned. It happened to us.

It is time for our generation to write its own history. Others are already making a start. Over the past year, our incomparably braver contemporaries in North Africa and the Maghreb have spearheaded the Arab Spring, rising up to overthrow a string of authoritarian governments once thought unassailable. Their courage and idealism has seemed to light a fire in the minds of youth across the world. The youthful protestors of Tunisia, Egypt, Libya and elsewhere have shown how no injustice can last forever if only enough people join together to oppose it. To see their movements for democracy is to feel the same uncynical enchantment Wordsworth felt when he witnessed the French Revolution: *Bliss was it in that dawn to be alive* ...

Yet, if we are to go beyond romanticism and become a generation that achieves social change, we would also do well to remember the advice of the revolutionary thinker Antonio Gramsci: optimism of the will, pessimism of the intellect.[5] The Arab Spring should instil in us a sense of agency, but offers few insights into the problems our generation faces in the UK. In place of tyrannies, we face the tyranny of No Alternative – to the advance of the market, to the inexorable destruction of the biosphere, to the unchallenged accumulation of wealth by an older elite. Having no sense of a viable alternative to the status quo saps the will to change anything. In the words of the late historian Tony Judt, 'We know from experience that politics, like nature, abhors a vacuum. After twenty wasted years it is time to start again. What is to be done?'[6] What is to be done is the subject of this book.

The authors of this book are – with one or two exceptions – members of the generation born since 1979. Some of us are studying for degrees; others work in the third sector, in business, in medicine, as journalists, or for higher education. We share a disillusionment over the way that politics has been conducted in Britain over the past thirty years, and the apparent breakdown of the social contract between generations. But we also share a desire to come up with better alternatives; not just to say *no* to the old ways of things, but emphatically *yes* to new solutions.

As Edward Kennedy once wrote, 'the answers of one generation become the questions of the next'.[7] Our questioning begins by interrogating the legacy of our parents in allowing the ascent of neoliberalism. How, ask **Adam Ramsay** and **Peter McColl** in their chapter, did the generation in power let financial markets become so huge and so loosely regulated that they were able to crash the economy in 2008? How has society come to meekly tolerate Edwardian levels of inequality? The reasons, they argue, lie in the erosion of community bonds and social responsibility – the loss of a collective stake in society. We need to rebuild society from the bottom up, allowing people far more say over the decisions that shape their lives – and far greater democratic control over flows of mobile capital.

Yet the consequences of the crash mean that we as a generation already face a bleaker outlook than that of our parents. Six years of austerity and a decade of stagnation await us: bliss, indeed. To come to terms with this fact, asks **Noel Hatch**, do we need to learn to be poorer before we become more powerful? Only by discarding some of our inherited illusions can we start to imagine a different future;

only by questioning our assumptions about social status and material aspiration can we aspire to a better world.

Another given for our generation is the creep of the market into every aspect of our lives – even, writes **Matthew Cheeseman**, into the way we spend our leisure-time. The 'night-time economy' of booze, bars and clubs dominates the lives of young people far more than it did thirty years ago; and whilst we're familiar with the damage binge-drinking causes to our health, we're less conscious of the ailments it conceals. Getting shitfaced, in short, is no compensation for a shit job, and we shouldn't let a profusion of happy hours blind us to the con of consumerism, nor the lack of decent employment.

Yet, as **Ben Little** warns, becoming fixated on markets risks missing the bigger problem: one of ownership. Certainly we should defend public services against marketisation – but we need also to go on the offensive, calling out how 'free' markets have actually resulted in obscene concentrations of wealth and corporate oligopolies. Previous governments have tried to sell us 'shareowning democracy', swiftly followed by 'property-owning democracy' – yet the former has proved incapable of holding companies to account, whilst the latter has led to a huge housing bubble, a booming buy-to-let sector, and a generation stuck on the bottom rung of the property ladder. A better alternative, Little argues, would be to explore collective forms of ownership – for both the housing we live in and the companies we work in.

More fundamental still than markets or ownership is the growth economy. As **Charlie Young** and **Rina Kuusipalo** argue in their chapter, achieving prosperity within a world of ecological limits will require nothing less than an alternative economics. 2012 will see world leaders gather again in Rio, twenty years after the original Earth Summit, to discuss the future of the planet that we stand to inherit. Rather than let this moment go the same way as the Copenhagen climate talks, the Summit should be an occasion to redefine the guiding stars of our economic system – placing wellbeing, rather than wealth, and equality rather than trickle-down growth, at the heart of our economies.

There is no denying, however, that where two years ago all eyes were on the climate crisis, that focus has since shifted almost wholly to the economic malaise. Writing in the first *Radical Future* book, Joss Garman warned of 'carbon fatigue' and the 'risk of loss of momentum' following Copenhagen. Those warnings appear to have been borne out – but so, too, has his call for greens to move 'beyond activism as usual.' Writing in this volume, **Richard George** asks whether we can build an environmentalism as if climate change didn't matter. Perhaps, he argues, it's time to stop talking about saving society from climate change and start talking about the sort of society we want to save. By building new alliances and not obsessing about carbon alone, we might also find we can better tackle the root causes of global warming.

Feminism, like environmentalism, is a movement that appears to come in waves – and the UK is currently seeing a resurgence of public interest in feminism. That doesn't mean, argues **Ray Filar**, that feminism or the problems it sought to solve ever went away – nor that its latest incarnation is necessarily equipped to move the debate on. To construct a feminism for the next generation, we need fresh ideas. Some of the most interesting of these come from queer politics: challenging the norms of heterosexual monogamy, questioning rigid gender categories, and learning from the queer movement's successes in reclaiming formerly pejorative terms.

Though 2011 saw movements for democracy spread across North Africa, in the UK a fairer voting system was kicked into the long grass for another generation by the No vote in the AV Referendum. The result has been cause for despondency amongst democracy campaigners, recounts **Becky Luff** – but now the dust has settled, it's time to move on and look for new opportunities to extend and enhance democratic practices on a local, transnational and global level. As the EU tries to move towards tighter fiscal union, plugging its democratic deficit will become ever-more important. And as the Occupy movements show, there is a deep-seated yearning for greater democratic accountability at a global level: whether through decentralised Peoples' Assemblies, or – one day – a directly-elected UN Parliamentary Assembly.

New ideas are vital, but without new ways of organising we will find ourselves at a loss to implement them. Six of the contributions in this book consider how we can best mobilise for collective action.

The winter of 2010-11 saw a reinvigoration of student activism, with huge protests against the trebling of tuition fees and loss of Educational Maintenance Allowance. The nature of these protests, and where the student protestors go from here, is the subject of an exchange between **Guy Aitchison** and **Jeremy Gilbert**.

But unless young progressives break out of the activist bubble, warns **George Gabriel**, we will never build the broad-based movement we want to see. A suspicion of established institutions like trade unions and churches, and a propensity to organise only with other young activists, risks fatally diluting our power. Community organising, by contrast, offers a route to construct powerful alliances between diverse interest groups and agitate for common action. Aspiring radicals can learn much from the work of London Citizens – still more so from the examples of teachers, unionists, priests and shopkeepers who have patiently and determinedly driven forward campaigns like the Living Wage.

Contending with entrenched power requires raising up a countervailing set of forces – what **Tim Gee**, in his chapter, terms Counterpower. This can take various forms: as ideas designed to undermine orthodox thinking; as strikes, boycotts and other means of pressing economic sanctions; or as 'Physical Counterpower' – acts of civil disobedience in defiance of the governing regime. Learning from historic struggles helps us choose which tactic is most appropriate for a given situation. It should also ward us off thinking that only one strategy can ever win, or romanticising only the most revolutionary of actors. Our parents had Che and 1968; but we are the *children* of the children of that revolution, and ought to learn something from how the baby boomers' ideals faded with passing.[8]

Modern protest is often carnivalesque, mixing rave and revolution. But as **Paolo Gerbaudo** observes from spending time with the Spanish *indignados*, the uprisings of 2011 have been distinguished by their relative sobriety – a new seriousness that seems a hallmark of protest in the age of austerity. Where previously Madrid's Puerta del Sol was thronged with young revellers drinking *calimocho*, the young rebels of 15 May have eschewed alcohol and drugs – demonstrating their discipline and helping a wider public, who may not buy into youthful or countercultural lifestyles, to feel included.

That doesn't mean we shouldn't have fun when we protest. As the influential community organiser Saul Alinsky said, 'if your people aren't having a ball doing it, there is something very wrong with the tactic'.[9] Humour, fun and verve have all been central to the tactics of UK Uncut, the most vibrant and effective new direct action group to emerge in Britain over the past year. UK Uncut participant **Chris Coltrane** relates what worked for the group and what didn't – and what others can learn to replicate their success. And comic strip artist extraordinaire **John Miers** tells the story of UK Uncut over six beautifully-drawn pages.

As Occupy has shown, simply creating space for discussion can be hugely powerful in itself. But sometimes it's also useful to pin down what changes we would make upon attaining power – so a spread of chapters in this book discuss potential policies.

Though seldom the concern of young activists, pensions are one of the most obvious forms of contract between generations, and form the subject of **Craig Berry**'s chapter. The current set of reforms to the state pension will oblige us to save more for our futures. This isn't all bad, but we need to be aware of how the institutional set-up of the pensions system has also become tilted out of our favour. Since Thatcher, we have moved towards individualised rather than collective provision of pensions – where we finance our own retirements rather than benefit from a risk-sharing, redistributive social safety net. Meanwhile, with wages stagnating, and with globalisation driving a trend towards more 'flexible' (i.e. less reliable) jobs, our generation often has less from which to save up in the first place. If the state is going to further individualise pension provision, then it has to guarantee decent employment opportunities for the young.

Indeed, gone are the days when the government could rely simply on expanding education to get young people jobs, argue **Martin Allen** and **Patrick Ainley**. In fact, many of today's generation under 30 are 'overqualified and underemployed' – possessed of a shining array of qualifications but all-too-often saddled with student debt and struggling to find employment commensurate with their education. Allen and Ainley suggest we have to go beyond the 'education, education, education' mantra of the Blair years and recognise we can't simply educate our way out of recession: more interventionist policies to directly support youth employment are now needed.

One way of making education better suited to real-life challenges is explored by **Jamie Audsley** and **Jim O'Connell**. In their chapter, told through the eyes of a pupil at an imaginary co-operative school, they suggest how pre-16 schooling might better connect to local communities, teach life skills, and foster shared values of creativity, inclusion and belonging.

For those considering how to embark on a career that combines both ethics and profits, social enterprise can seem an attractive option. As **David Floyd** writes, social enterprise emerged as an archetypal 'third-way' initiative, as Blairite policy wonks sought to split the difference between encouraging entrepreneurialism and delivering social goals beyond the bottom line. Whilst the sector continues to perform strongly and attracts a younger and more diverse workforce than traditional companies, social enterprise overall still lacks a coherent definition, and could learn more from the history of the co-operative and workplace democracy movements whose decline it has sought to plug.

The past year has seen defenders of the NHS rally against the Coalition's proposed reforms. Public financing of healthcare must be defended as the fairest and most efficient way of delivering healthy citizens, write **Guppi Bola** and **Christo Albor**. But if we are to improve health prospects for all, we need to go on the offensive. Health policy isn't just about the structure of the healthcare system, they suggest, but is also about the overarching level of inequality in society. Creating a healthier society will require challenging the gross income inequalities that have emerged over the past thirty years.

2011 was also of course the year that saw Rupert Murdoch's News International rocked to its core by the phone-hacking scandal, which led to renewed calls for fundamental reform of the British media. But this once-in-a-generation chance for change faces an uphill struggle against vested interests. **Tim Holmes** takes apart the arguments of the apologists for the status quo and shows that, whatever cause we give primacy to, media reform has to be our second priority.

Lastly, if we are to get serious about defending the interests of all future generations against today's short-termist impulses, we need to represent these interests in our politics. **Kirsty Schneeberger** outlines the legal options for an Ombudsman or Parliamentary Commissioner for Future Generations – whose remit would entail speaking up for future generations on decisions which would affect them, from climate policy to pensions reform.

★

To be inspired by others' political struggles – whether the French revolutionaries of 1789 or the Arab revolutionaries of 2011 – is to kindle a spark of hope in dark times. But to generate heat from these sparks needs a real belief that alternatives exist to the current way of things. Our generation has grown up during a period of stagnant consensus in British politics. We have been told – both explicitly and implicitly, through the choices on offer – that 'there is no alternative' to the spread of markets, rising inequality and escalating ecological crises. This lie is now crumbling.

The generation that has grown up in the time since the 'end of history' is starting to write its own history. We have begun to fill the moral and political vacuum of the past thirty years with our own alternatives.

It falls to our generation to question the answers of the previous one, to mix idealism and pragmatism in generating a fresh consensus better suited to the challenges of our era. For many, it is assuredly not bliss to be alive in these times. But to be young, it is at least to know certainty: that we can build a far, far better world than the one we have inherited.

Clare Coatman has worked on a range of projects within the field of democratic reform, including Yes to Fairer Votes and the Convention on Modern Liberty. As one of the founders of Take Back Parliament, Clare is an experienced activist, originally as a school student spokesperson during the Iraq War protests. She is currently Fundraising and Marketing Manager for openDemocracy.

Guy Shrubsole is a writer, researcher and activist. He is Director of Public Interest Research Centre, an independent charity that works towards a more sustainable society. In 2011, he co-authored *Think Of Me As Evil? Opening the ethical debates in advertising*, a study on the social and environmental impacts of advertising described by Ed Mayo as 'the best written report on any social cause for many a year'. Previously, he worked on climate change policy for the Department of the Environment, Food and Rural Affairs, and for New Zealand's Ministry of Agriculture.

Notes

1. William Wordsworth, *The Prelude*, Book Eleven (1799), London: Macmillan, 1888.

2. Francis Fukuyama, *The End of History and the Last Man,* New York: Free Press, 1992.
3. United Nations Framework Convention on Climate Change, 1992.
4. OK, this chronology isn't applicable to everyone in our generation, but it's the median age...
5. Antonio Gramsci, *Prison Notebooks* (1929), Columbia University Press, 2011, p.175.
6. Tony Judt, *Ill Fares the Land,* London: Penguin, 2011.
7. Edward Kennedy, address to the 1980 Democratic National Convention.
8. Though our generation might also learn something from the politicised songwriters of the Sixties. Come back, T-Rex, all is forgiven.
9. Saul Alinsky, *Rules for Radicals,* New York: Random House, 1971.

Rebuilding society from the bottom up

Adam Ramsay and Peter McColl

The rapid flow of money around the world is good for almost no one. More specifically, profit – the money skimmed by our employers from the value of the work we do – has been misused. Rather than being invested productively in our communities, it has increasingly been handed to financiers who send it off to join the 'electronic herd'– thundering around the globe to bet on the changing values of whichever financial products are bubbling this week.[1] The turbulence the stampede creates crashes currencies and inflates prices. In 2008, it crushed the global economy. So, how do we corral this herd?

When Britain's welfare state was built, it was universal: services were not means tested. It is no coincidence that countries with welfare states solely for the poor have poor welfare states. If only 10 per cent use something, the other 90 per cent won't understand it, so they will allow it to wither away. If everyone depends on a service, everyone will work to defend it: job seekers' allowance is attacked, whilst we demand weekly bin collection. Universalism made almost everyone – Labour and Tory – a social democrat.

But Mrs Thatcher found a way to break that bind. She gave a generation the 'Right to Buy' council houses. Nationalised industries were sold, and more and more people became shareholders – became capitalists. She called it 'property owning democracy'. Whereas people used to have a stake in public and civic institutions, now they had a stake in the market – if house or share prices went up, they'd feel richer. If they collapsed, they'd feel poorer. And so the middle moved to the right because they believed their interests now aligned with the wealthy.

Similarly, she introduced a more 'flexible' labour market. People moved more from job to job, becoming less and less likely to know their neighbours. We were turned from citizens to consumers, encouraged not to look after each other, but to covet gizmos. She removed significant powers from local councils so that we would make fewer decisions as communities, and unleashed record inequality which ripped us apart from each other. If the welfare state is how we organise our love for each other, then Thatcher demanded divorce. She declared there was no such thing as society, then attempted to make it so.

In 2008 Thatcherite economies collapsed. In the following wave of protests around the world, demands varied. But as well as the macro-economic demands you would expect, one call was consistent: 'real democracy'. And it is perhaps through true participation that we can re-build not just our economies, but also the sense of social solidarity severed by neoliberalism.

Latin America, 'socialism for the twenty-first century' and participatory budgeting

If there is anywhere in the world that might claim to be moving towards such 'real democracy', then it might be the city of Porto Alegre, Brazil. Perhaps here we can begin to understand how we can rebuild the society that Mrs Thatcher worked so hard to abolish, and how to ensure that surplus value left from our work remains rooted in our communities. And perhaps here too we can begin to find ways to build a system which protects itself – a system which ensures that people have the faith, and the understanding, to fight for it.

Porto Alegre's $200 million budget is written not by the mayor, but by its citizens. Each year, thousands gather in January at events across the city to begin the process of discussing priorities and allocating funds. Everyone is welcome. They listen to each other, and to various experts. They consider options. And then, after discussion, delegation, reflection and negotiation, they decide between them how to spend their taxes. They've gone through this process every year since 1989.

Over the last two decades this example has been taken up across Latin America. Today, millions of people in thousands of cities come together to similarly work out how to allocate their resources. The rapid expansion perhaps speaks for itself – it is so popular because it is remarkably successful. People, if they put their minds to it, are intelligent and creative. They are the experts in their communities, so they make better choices about their communities.

If we look only at policy outcomes, then the success is remarkable. A World Bank study into Porto Alegre's budget process showed real success in tackling the deep poverty in the city.[2]

But the decisions made through this process are not its only outcome. Because intrinsic to it is a process of education and of empowerment: as people come together with their community to discuss their respective needs and priorities, they get to know each other. They learn about how and why various services are delivered. They build bonds of social solidarity.

In 2005, Josh Lerner and Daniel Schugurensky conducted in depth interviews with forty people from the Argentinean town of Rosario, which uses participatory budgeting processes.[3] They wanted to find out what the impact had been not on the decisions that were made, but on the people making them. The following quotes are from those interviews:

Before I thought: why should I care about some traffic light if I knew my thoughts wouldn't count? Now, because I think my idea will be considered, I'm more motivated to pay attention to problems in the city and see what I can do about them. For

example, now if I'm driving alongside a sidewalk in bad repair, I
see the sidewalk as a problem to fix. (Simona)
    I learned that there are all sorts of neighbourhoods, with very
different needs. (Carlos)

The academics conclude that the process very clearly created more
socially conscious, 'better' citizens, aware of the needs of those
around them, better able to articulate their own.

    In the UK in 2008, the *Sun* reported a poll in which people
voted 'benefit scroungers' the most annoying thing in Britain.[4]
Whilst much of the perception of mis-claimed benefits is driven by
the political right and the tabloid media, it is also made possible by
a society in which those paying taxes and those claiming benefits
don't know each other. And a key way for people to find out
which of their perceptions are accurate and which aren't is
through learning – as Carlos did – about the needs of their
neighbours. And once these lessons have been learned, perhaps it
would be harder for budgets to be cut. People who have a
conception of why each pound is needed by someone, why it all
matters – as opposed to people who are passive consumers of
public services, being asked to stand up and defend organisations
they don't really understand – are much more likely to protect
expenditure. So, just as Thatcher dismantled society and gave us
all a stake in the market, perhaps we need to re-build society by
giving ourselves a stake in each other?

    But whilst it is there that it has had most success, participatory
budgeting isn't unique to Latin America.

    Leith is the old dock on the edge of Edinburgh, famous as the set
of the film *Trainspotting*. In 2010, the local community managed to
persuade the Edinburgh City Council to hand £16,600 of
development funding over to them. They held an event – '£eith
Decides'. Hundreds of local people came, pitched community
project ideas, and voted on who would receive what.

    Many great projects received welcome cash. But perhaps more

significantly, the community understood why the cash was needed – how it would benefit everyone to spend it in this way. As one attendee said afterwards:

> Many of the projects – African drumming for unemployed youths, cookers for drug addicts – are the sorts of things the *Daily Mail* would lambast. But no one left complaining about them – once they had had the need for these projects explained in detail, they left wishing they could have given them more.

Of course, this was only a small amount of money. But it showed that when given control over such decisions, people are more likely to support such expenditure – to see the need.

And it is perhaps heading north from Edinburgh that we find the UK's most exciting examples of community empowerment.

Community land ownership, community renewables, and the Highlands of Scotland

The population of the Highlands of Scotland have for centuries suffered at the whim of their landlords and of the global markets. In the eighteenth century Robert Burns intervened, writing to the Earl of Breadalbane, as Beelzebub, 'congratulating' him on his murderous ways:

> They, an' be damn'd! what right hae they
> To meat, or sleep, or light o' day?
> Far less – to riches, pow'r, or freedom,
> But what your lordship likes to gie them?
> (from 'Address of Beelzebub', Robert Burns, 1786)

By the 1880s, a campaign of crofters' civil disobedience put the issue of land rights centre stage, and five MPs from the Crofters' party were elected; they managed to secure the Crofting Act of 1886.

But their problems didn't go away, and in 2003, the Scottish Parliament passed the Land Reform Act. Among other things, this finally gave crofting communities some right to buy their land – as a few already had.

Perhaps the most famous example is the first community buy-out – the Island of Eigg. In 1997, the inhabitants of this small isle managed to mobilise enough support and funds to oust their absentee landlord, and buy their mountain in the sea. The best known book about the buy-out, written by one of the founder members of the Eigg Trust, Alastair McIntosh, is tellingly called *Soil and Soul – people versus corporate power*.[5] In it McIntosh draws clear links – as the people of Rosario in Argentina did – between economic control and the re-building of community values.

If you visit Eigg, it's easy to see this for yourself. When I was there in summer 2009, the entrance to the community café had a large display drawn by local children. It explained that the sea-birds were disappearing because the fish were going; and that the fish were going because the sea was getting warmer; and that the sea was getting warmer because of carbon emissions; and so, it explained, this might be a small community on the very corner of the British Isles, but it would do its bit. The building is shadowed by a row of wind turbines. The burns on the island each have micro-hydro power, and between 2008 and 2010 they reduced their carbon emissions from domestic fuel by 45 per cent. In their shop, nestled between bright white bread and tins of baked beans, you find jars of Fairtrade Palestinian olives – an expression of solidarity.

The café, the wind turbines, the hydro-power – all have been investments since the buy-out. In simple economic terms, it has been a success. But while communities across the Highlands are opposing wind turbines thrust upon them, the people of Eigg have, through the process of coming together and planning together, taken on broader global needs. And so they have insisted that they will lead Britain's low carbon revolution.

And this is not an isolated example. Look at almost any of the

Highland community buy-outs, and you will find exciting, outward-looking projects – almost all powered with community-owned renewables. The process of bringing communities together to make real economic decisions together seems to do something: it seems to help us remember what communities are about – to rebuild our love for one another.

But both cases help with another problem: what to do with our 'electronic herd'. After the Great Depression, a series of international regulations were introduced to stop another crash. But a key failure of these regulations was political – there was no organised group who would prioritise defending them. And so they were slowly frittered away.

They must be restored, but we surely need to find another way to protect our children from a bankers' crash. And so, what if instead of just regulating, we also say this: we don't hand the capital from our work to a small elite and then try to stop them gambling with it too much. We give it roots – we build communities with the capacity to discuss and decide where to invest next, and then watch as those communities demand that the value created by their work is invested as they wish. Because if there is a lesson from the credit crunch, it is surely that we cannot trust elites to invest our wealth. And if the lessons from the Highlands, and the lessons from Latin America, teach us anything, it is surely this: when communities come together, they make wise choices, they stand up for each other, they learn from each other. Because we are humans, and we love each other.

Of course, the barrios of Rossario and the Highlands of Scotland may seem remote to the average Westerner. But if we are to re-build an economy trashed by decades of individualism, then we must first re-build community and society. After Bolivian social movements had finally ended decades of enforced neoliberalism, one activist discussed the process they went through to re-build their country. They didn't just have to develop better institutions and create fairer laws. They had to 'glue society back together from the bottom up'. That, surely, is the challenge we now face.

Adam Ramsay is co-editor of the blog Bright Green, activism manager for student network People & Planet, and involved in a number of campaign and activist groups in Oxford and nationally.

Peter McColl is co-editor of the blog Bright Green, a community activist in Edinburgh and works for a charity.

Notes

1. Thomas Friedman, *The Lexus and the Olive Tree*, Farrar, Straus and Giroux 1999.
2. Deepti Bhatnagar, Animesh Rathore, Magüi Moreno Torres and Parameeta Kanungo, *Participatory Budgeting in Brazil*, Indian Institute of Management and World Bank: http://siteresources.worldbank.org/INTEMPOWERMENT/Resources/14657_Partic-Budg-Brazil-web.pdf
3. Josh Lerner and Daniel Schugurensky, 'Learning citizenship and democracy through participatory budgeting: The case of Rosario, Argentina', conference paper presented at *Democratic Practices as Learning Opportunities*, Columbia University, New York: www.linesofflight.net/work/rosario_pb_columbia.pdf
4. Sue Marsh, 'Ed Miliband and the "Cheats" and "Shirkers"', Diary of a Benefit Scrounger: http://diaryofabenefitscrounger.blogspot.com/2011/06/ed-miliband-and-cheats-and-shirkers.html
5. Alastair McIntosh, *Soil and Soul: people versus corporate power*, Aurum Press 2001

Further reading: *The Pedagogy of the Oppressed*

Learning to be poorer yet more powerful

Noel Hatch

The generation born after 1979 has barely been given a glimpse of an alternative to a consumerism in which our identities are shaped by what we consume, and our work life is given over to the gods of economic efficiency. From education to advertising, our coming of age has been dominated by the interests of those in power – not only to institutionalise our place in society, but also as a way of maintaining the status quo.

It's in the friction between what we've been taught to expect and how we're starting to understand the reality of our situation that our generation can begin to take back its future. That's why in this chapter I'll explore what we've been brought up to believe and what we experience; how we see ourselves as a generation and how we see the world around us; and what strategies we are starting to use to cope with the shock of shattered illusions.

If we are going to imagine a future that we can claim as our own, we also need to explore different socio-cultural practices where we can find the most creative ways of opening ourselves up to new ways of being together. To do this we need to tell stories that help create shared meaning for our generation, and learn from those whom the powerful never acknowledge. I'll then look at how we can make sense of the world we live in to understand how we need to change – rehearsing new ways of living to open up people's imaginations and creating new social roles that help us become more powerful.

'You don't choose the filter, it chooses you': What we've been brought up to believe and what we experience

Before we look at how we can rethink the way we live together, let's go back to first principles to understand the difference between the myths we believed in and the reality we're faced with.

In economic terms, our 'spending power' has disguised the fact that consumerism has strangled the capacity for our generation to learn how to make the economy work for us. Instead, we 'indebt' ourselves in the addictive warmth of readymade identities.

This is reinforced by a general failure of democracy: we don't have time to question how much vested interests have perpetrated the myth that 'there is no alternative' to consumer capitalism. It's through the media that the ways we've been brought up to see the world are falling apart the most visibly. It has 'manufactured consent' so well that we've only just stopped to think how 'unreal' these myths are in the face of our everyday lives.[1]

Ironically, if there's a channel that manufactures consent most addictively, it's social media – the channel we have grown up with – where we re-tweet consent without realising. The experiences we consume online are manufactured too, with our feelings (and photos) packaged back to us as Facebook ads for how we should live our lives.

Even when people find solutions that could get us out of this consumerist paradigm, we've been socialised by it to such an extent that we find it 'really hard for people to ask for and receive help from our neighbours. We understand charity, but genuine reciprocity is harder'.[2]

As influential sociologist Zygmunt Bauman sums up: 'the gap between the right of self-assertion and the capacity to control the social settings which render such self-assertion feasible or unrealistic seems to be the main contradiction of fluid modernity'.[3] In short, we cannot create political, economic or social alternatives without starting with a change in how our generation sees the world.

'Snakes and ladders': How we see ourselves as a generation and how we see the world around us

As consumers, we've built our identities out of the brands that we identify with. We perform different roles to cope with the situations we're faced with.

We get tempted to publicise our private emotions and relegate our family and friends to cameo roles while we concern ourselves with the ups and downs of celebrities to fill the void of emptiness and loneliness. We try to act out a role, convinced that what we consume defines how successful we are; how worthy we are of attention.

In some ways it feels like the only response possible. We prefer the conformism of running the rat race like a hamster on a spinning wheel. We prefer the quick fixes of consuming, because we fear freedom – to be what we want to be rather than what we think others want us to be.

But what happens in a crisis, when we're plunging off the cliff of affluence? When the illusion that 'we're all middle class' comes crashing down, and the reality of not being able to keep up with the Joneses becomes an exercise in futility?[4]

We forget that the concept of class was based on a more visceral relationship that people had with the economy, with politics and with their communities. People knew where they stood and where they'd end up. Our generation, on the other hand, has always been taught to climb the social ladder higher than our families had ever been before. But we got 'snaked', and have even ended further down that we started off.

It's difficult to know what's worse: expecting not to have the things your parents had, and preparing yourself for alternatives to getting a job, a house or even a degree – or assuming everything's going to be OK, until you realise that your dreams have been privatised, getting yourself into debt to even grab a slice of them back.

Coping with the shock of shattered illusions

How we cope with this shock will affect not just how we can build a better future, but whether we can conceive of a better future at all. As a generation, we are not all coping in the same way. We move interchangeably between egocentrism, altruism, apathy and even alienation, depending on how difficult we find it to cope with the shock of not living the life we expected. This is why the social contract is so brittle in our hands.

Perhaps it will be the shared experience of suffering from precarious living situations that will change the expectations we have of life. To put it bluntly, do we need to learn to cope with getting poorer before we can start to become more powerful?

In order to change what we've been conditioned to think, and how we've been conditioned to act, we need to learn how to create new behaviours and ways of living that foreshadow alternatives.

Putting our generation on the map

To do this, we need to more fully observe how people live their lives around us, to better make sense of unmet needs and create new symbols of belonging for our generation. Traditionally it's been governments who've invested in creating these symbols to legitimise their power over people. They commissioned maps to visualise boundaries, censuses to classify the population and museums to maintain the nation's memory.

What's changed now is that our generation is creating ways of mapping which don't visualise boundaries, but rather help people make the connections between different perspectives on issues they care about.[5] They don't classify the population based on what people are defined by but, alternatively, get people to sketch what they feel in public spaces to measure the wellbeing of their neighbourhood.[6] They don't use museums to maintain an official memory but instead get people to make things together that show people how they'd like to connect with other groups in their community.[7]

Occupy the change you want to see

As well as understanding how our peers are coping with the disparity between the future we were promised and the very different experience we are having, what if we 'rehearsed' new realities that helped people imagine different ways of living in society?

There are already examples out there. We could learn from the Human Library, which 'enables groups to break stereotypes by challenging the most common prejudices in a positive and humorous manner';[8] or from the 'big society bail in', which gets people to have 'read-ins' in banks to foreshadow the future if we bailed out public services rather than big banks.[9] You might think these examples are superficial considering the challenges we face, but 'fiction becomes reality when people choose to invest in it'.[10] This is a lesson we can learn from the Occupy movement. They don't just ask for the change they want to see, they actually start being that change – making decisions collectively, sharing resources and creating spaces for people to develop ideas.[11]

Through these sorts of activities we can start creating new behaviours in such a way that they change people's perception of society. But, just as gangs create new codes to define themselves, we too need to think of new ways to define ourselves as a generation. If 'fast food' could change the script for having a meal, or if campaigners on disability rights could develop a social model that's transformed the way we see the relationship between public services and its users, we can create scripts to change the way we expect to make a living.

Transforming behaviours in the open air

It's important we understand 'how radical changes often come when we find a new way to make room for something old'.[12] As social media theorist Clay Shirky says, 'transformation in society doesn't happen when it adopts new tools, it happens when it adopts new behaviours'.[13] So how can we best use the behaviours that digital technology has given us without needing to rely on its infrastructure? Will the 'human microphone' used in the occupations be the next generation's 're-tweet'?[14] Will the 'complaints choirs' spreading across the world be the next generation's 'feedback form'?[15] What all of these have in common is that they put digital concepts out into the open air, and in contact with the senses that technology finds it so difficult to recognise or value.

New ways of relating with groups can be created when people experience realities they haven't been brought up to expect, particularly where third-world conditions start appearing in 'developed' societies.[16] That's why we can learn how to live together in ways we hadn't thought possible by rediscovering the people and places we interact with through different eyes – for example by going on a tour with refugees or migrants to discover the nooks and crannies of cities, or showing people how they can use art to challenge people's prejudices.[17] Indeed, the more we immerse ourselves in different backgrounds and experiences, the more we can cope with what society throws at us and move our generation from a solitary 'I wish this was' to a collective 'I wish we could'.

To conclude, if we need to question ourselves first, we can make use of new technologies to understand the world around us. If we need to create new ways of living, we can start creating self-fulfilling prophecies to open up people's imagination to new possibilities. If we need to create new meaning for our generation, we can start telling the stories that foreshadow a better future. If we need to find new ways of seeing the world, we can learn from those the world never acknowledges.

Noel Hatch is Co-Chair of the Transeuropa Cooperative. He has designed over fifty activities and workshops to support people to develop creative campaigning skills in public spaces; and is Youth Chair of Compass and co-founder of Visual Camp & Campaign Camp. He blogs at www.wedowhatwesee.org.

Notes

1. Paul Mason, 'Murdoch: the network defeats the hierarchy': www.bbc.co.uk/news/business-14093772.
2. Local Circles, 'Get involved': http://localcircles.org/get-involved/.
3. Zygmunt Bauman, *Liquid Modernity*, Polity 2000.
4. Steve Doughty 'So we're all middle class now': www.dailymail.co.uk/news/article-1368162/Seven-10-Brits-middle-class.html.
5. Noel Hatch, 'Visual Camp': www.wedowhatwesee.org/?tag=visualcamp.
6. Emily Wilkinson and Laura Sorvala 'Come to Your Senses': www.mindfulmaps.com/2011/05/come-to-your-senses-mapping-experience/.
7. Tessy Britton, 'Travelling Pantry': www.tessybritton.com/51057/Social-Spaces-Travelling-Pantry
8. Human Library, 'What is the Human Library?': http://humanlibrary.org/what-is-the-living-library.html
9. UK Uncut, 'Big Society Bail In': http://bit.ly/nUzRH5
10. Vinay Gupta, 'Creativity and Crisis': http://blip.tv/the-hexayurt-project/creativity-and-crisis-vinay-gupta-at-the-thursday-club-goldsmiths-london-02011-09-28-5604593.
11. www.bankofideas.org.uk/welcome/
12. Dougald Hine, 'The University Project': http://dougald.posterous.com/the-university-project-my-tedx-london-talk
13. Clay Shirky, Here Comes Everybody: The Power of Organizing Without Organizations, Penguin 2008.
14. #occupyws, 'How it works by Occupy Wall Street': www.youtube.com/watch?v=xIK7uxBSAS0
15. Complaints Choirs, 'Complaints Choirs: www.complaintschoir.org/
16. Paul Mason, 'In Steinbeck's footsteps: America's middle-class underclass': www.bbc.co.uk/news/world-us-canada-14296682.
17. For examples see: Biciclettata Tragitti migranti: www.euroalter.com/festival/bologna/biciclettata-tragitti-migranti; 'JR's TED Prize wish: Use art to turn the world inside out': www.ted.com/talks/jr_s_ted_prize_wish_use_art_to_turn_the_world_inside_out.html; 'Promenade urbaine dans le Paris multicultural': www.euroalter.com/festival/paris/promenade-urbaine-dans-le-paris-multiculturel.

In the dead of the night

Matthew Cheeseman

When my aunt and uncle visited Cheltenham in the late 1980s, they stepped out on Saturday night to see the town. They found a few pubs and nothing much beyond a cold welcome. The place, as my aunt said, was dead. Twenty-five years later and Cheltenham is drawing 20,000 weekend punters from the region between Bristol and Birmingham. People go on their stag and hen nights to Cheltenham, joining a lively student night-life catering for the University of Gloucestershire, which also developed in this period. There are around 125 restaurants, 87 bars and pubs and 14 night clubs in the centre.[1] It is by no means Babylon, but this growth is indicative of the changes that many British towns experienced in the development of what is now known as their 'night-time economy'. Certainly, when my aunt and uncle's children choose to visit Cheltenham as young adults, they do so because it is decidedly not dead.

Wandering through its pedestrianised zone in the early hours of Sunday morning can be a thrilling and visceral trip. The bray of banter competes with the chants of celebration, echoing off the ubiquitous hunched riot vans. An early anthropologist would detect elements of a rite of passage, and indeed it is hard to resist sensing something natural and vital about these urban binges. Many of us can attest to the life-affirming potential and the possibilities for friendship that the night-time economy opens up. Going out is empowering, a claiming of space via the irresistible, joyous thrills of getting out of your head. And yet other forces are roused when high spirits are engaged. All of us have witnessed the danger of the night, when gas bubbles from the churning muck of booze, suddenly bursting into eruptions of assault, abuse, addiction. This bodily violence is inexcusable and raises important questions through which to think about Britain at night: why do we behave like this when we are supposedly relaxing from work? Many of us implicitly understand the attraction of such behaviour, especially when it is mediated through CCTV cameras into programmes which disguise their entertainment value as lurid social reportage. My grandmother never misses these weekly displays. Neither do my younger cousins. TV makes Victorian anthropologists of us all, horrified and yet fascinated, secretly recognising something of ourselves on the murky screen, in stories of our own construction.

This world was brought about only relatively recently. Significant legislation was passed under Tony Blair's premiership which developed further the Major government's challenge to 1990s rave culture, the last mass moment of UK youth. The key piece was the Licensing Act of 2003, which gave local authorities the freedom to design 'scripted' geographic areas for alcohol retailers and other night-time businesses, ranging from theatres to takeaways. Alcohol is this new zone's chief intoxicant and ruling commodity. As such it has been marketed in ways which have profoundly changed its consumption patterns, amongst both men and women, but especially the latter. A wide-scale popularisation of shots, shooters, alcopops and cocktails has occurred in the last twenty years, accompanying the normalisation of fancy dress and other play routines, alongside such so-called 'traditional drinking events' such as 'St Guinness Day'. When we go out it may feel like this has always been the way, but it has not. A round of shots would have been a rare event fifteen years ago, a Jägerbomb conceptually impossible.[2]

These developments are not specific to any age group, yet they have affected this generation more than any other, especially in regards to what the General Household Survey calls 'Increased Sessional Drinking', what might otherwise be known as bingeing. The firm dichotomy between 'staying in' and 'going out', second nature to many, solidified in this period. For many, 'going out' now implies a performance that begins in 'pre-drinking' at home, moves on to a 'pre-bar' before climaxing in a loss of reflexivity on the dance floor of a nightclub. It is something intimately tied to the notion of friendship, not to the way friends are made – despite its promises, the night-time economy rarely introduces people – but rather to the way friendship ties are performed: by going out. That is not to say, of course, that there is anything inherently wrong with these elements (alcohol consumption, music, dancing and being with friends); it is merely to comment that their current means of expression is a product of deregulation and absolutely infused with the cunning deductions of neoliberalism.

Pleasure is, of course, a perennial human concern, and this generation is no different in its desires from any other. However, as with many contemporary problems, the cultural rights decisively claimed in the 1960s (sexual, expressive, individual) have become progressively monetised by thirty-plus years of Thatcherism, to the point where they have begun to resemble not freedoms but prisons. The allure of William Burroughs' Interzone has been incorporated into the machine. At the heart of this transformation is a disillusionment with work – with what can be achieved – and a full embrace of hedonism, of living for the thrills and spills of the weekend. Work in deindustrialised Britain is, for many, temporary, transient and devoid of meaning or progression. Shitwork implies a beer, and as capital sloshes its shallow course, hedonism follows in a riptide that intensifies individuating and sexualising forces. We willingly court risk within this pull: it makes us feel vital and alive. The zone understands this all too well, and has developed to deliver it, at significant cost to public health and emergency services.[3]

Alcohol consumption has become a shadow metaphor for consumerism: the raised shot glass its official, totemic gesture. This serves to transform alienation into something more human and bearable – a pleasure well deserved and worked for – and yet one that is, at the same time, riven with compromise. For the night-time economy is a complex entity, and nowhere is cultural and social stratification more tangible than within the scripted pleasure zones of our towns and cities. Everyone knows which places to avoid and which places to queue for, the places that cater for 'people like them'. Processes of distinction abound: customers of one world glimpse customers of another over the bollards and *ad hoc* pissoirs that mark pedestrianised areas, only to meet each other in fast-food whirlpools.

Inside and outside these zones, in the off-license, semi-legal and illegal party scenes, the only factor that could be said to tie the entirety of this generation together is the desire to live for the moment, whether in a high street nightclub, a teknival or even in protest. We all carry a shard of rave UK, and reflect a vision of what could be: celebration, transcendence and communality. How to conceive of, serve and deliver this desire is an important question for our culture, and one that deserves careful consideration from anyone concerned about its evolution. For it is important to remember that the drugs *do* work, whether they are pints, pills, powder or just pure and simple performance. We need to lose a sense of ourselves and enter the gliding flow and the vacation from being this brings.

There is a coherent (and at times aptly incoherent) reading that a new society can emanate from such states, or at least be rejuvenated by them. It is an attractive idea, and an old one, which has developed significant criticisms. One of these is that, when the metaphorical 'third-eye' opens, it lets in two-way traffic. The market thus penetrates altered states through what is, essentially, a trapdoor for hegemony. This encourages the navel-gazing pursuit of personal pleasure in what amounts to a hedonistic treadmill compensating for meaningless, dehumanised work. To protect it from this perversion, group transcendence has been traditionally controlled and managed, often as a sacred rite. This is also the path that some contemporary counter-cultures have followed, with some success. Of course, in the night-time economy, the market holds the controlling interest in the apparatus that resolves the desire for group transcendence. For the mainstream then, capital takes full custody of the social relations that surround the very performance of going out. If friendship is maintained and enacted in the night-time economy, then friendship is maintained and performed in the market. In a climate which encourages it to be volatile, competitive and aggressive, there's no wonder that it enacts these conditions so visibly on its customers.

This neatly segues into the true genius of the night-time economy, encoded in the products it sells, which are a form of medicine, of relief from the very pressures of work, competition and consumerism that it also feeds. Shitwork, remember, deserves a beer, and no one ever gets depressed in Bakhtin's banterous fantasy.[4] With the rise of mental health problems in late capitalism, 'going out' can seem a form of self-medication, a sheep-dip in the anaesthetising alcohol of consumerism. No wonder the drugs are stronger in areas of economic deprivation. Class consciousness, meanwhile, is dampened by the altered states of consciousness of the pleasure factories, and their waste products of cold irony, cool distinction and self-satisfied banter. This feeds a collective amnesia of purpose which sees a future that cannot be grasped and can only be approached in repetitive bouts of education in an attempt to plateau out on a 'good job' and the lifestyle it affords.[5] Never being able to reach this vaunted Utopia leaves a big white space rippling through our futures, like a giant flag of surrender.

Hypersensitive to the 'drudgery of pleasure seeking',[6] I suffer from the paranoia of the researcher, and see it spreading everywhere, like a conspiracy of kicks. I was fascinated by the 2010 protests and the 2011 riots: was I too severe in recognising elements of the night-time economy in both? Indeed, 2010 seemed flush with flowing performance (*there was dancing in Parliament Square!*), whilst the riots were like a violent hangover from a never-ending, shit-faced night. Neither provided a coherent social vision beyond the thump of the bass and the flare of protest. Yet perhaps this is unfair: all protests contain elements of the carnivalesque, and it is easy to be critical of action in the moment.[7] I do wonder, however, whether the night-time economy does too good a job of satisfying, or at least sating, the desires of this generation. Cheltenham Spa is, after all, still thriving at night.

Indeed, in the first Radical Future book, Jeremy Gilbert commented – in reference to the defeat of socialism by neoliberalism – that 'a key consequence of this defeat is the absence of enduring institutions'.[8] It is my contention that new and pernicious institutions are evident in the night-time economy, plunging the long, cold fingers of consumerism into the performance of friendship, and making you thank it profusely for doing so. I am not proposing an age of personal austerity, nor attempting to devalue friendship. I am simply pressing awareness of the compromises that 'having a good time' often entails. For not only is the performance of friendship a means of cementing groups, it is also a way of imagining what those groups can be. By reclaiming this performance from the night-time economy, by wrestling ourselves from the communal compromises of transcendence and release, we take a step towards other possible futures. Only then will we be able to formulate new rituals capable of reanimating the dead.

Matthew Cheeseman is a contemporary folklorist based at the University of Sheffield. This chapter follows an article published in *Roundhouse Journal*, No. 2, April 2011, concerned with youth protest. He is currently preparing an ethnography of students at the University of Sheffield based on his doctoral research. In 2008/2009 he was selected to run an institutionally-funded research project by the University of Gloucestershire assessing alcohol intake amongst undergraduates. In 2008, he made two ethnographic films concerning youth pleasure, both of which were shown by SIEF in 2009.

Notes

1. Information on the Cheltenham night-time economy taken from the Cheltenham Community Safety Partnership 2008-2011 *Strategic Assessment*: www.cheltenhampartnership.org.uk.
2. For a good summary of these changes, see F. Measham, and K. Brain, '"Binge" Drinking, British Alcohol Policy and the New Culture of Intoxication', *Crime Media Culture*, 1 (3), 2005.
3. See House of Commons, *Health Committee First Report on Alcohol*, 2009: www.publications.parliament.uk/pa/cm200910/cmselect/ cmhealth/151/15102.htm
4. For a positive reading (at times cosmically so) of the pleasures of the body and the marketplace, see M. M. Bakhtin, *Rabelais and His World*, MIT Press 1968.
5. M. Allen, and P. Ainley, *Lost Generation? New Strategies for Youth and Education*, Continuum Publishing Corporation 2010.
6. S. Winlow, and S. Hall, *Violent Night: Urban Leisure and Contemporary Culture*, Berg 2006.
7. It is fascinating, however, to read of the self-imposed strictures of the Spanish *botellon sin alcohol* related by Paolo Gerbaudo elsewhere in this collection.
8. J. Gilbert, in B. Little (ed), *Radical Future – Politics for the Next Generation*, Lawrence & Wishart 2010, http://www.lwbooks.co.uk/ebooks/ radicalfuture.html, p121.

Forget markets: it's ownership that really matters

Ben Little

Neoliberalism, the political formation which has emphasised deregulated markets and financial capitalism for the last thirty years, is breaking down. It is in the throes of a final spasm of assertiveness, as the institutions it has co-opted seek to impose an austerity agenda across the world. Technocrats are replacing elected representatives and doctrinaire economists are becoming the new breed of politician, installed to perpetuate the interests of those who have benefitted most from the last three decades: the richest 1 per cent who have come to own a quarter of national wealth.[1] This is a new phase in world politics; and what replaces it – for better or worse – will not be the same as what has come before.

Thus, the strategies of the left in recent years may no longer be appropriate. Rather than simply oppose the marketisation of society, we need to shift our emphasis to challenging systems of ownership. Opposing market advance is wholly appropriate in some cases, such as healthcare and education; but ultimately this is a rearguard action – defending the last vestiges of a pre-1979 social settlement, rather than going on the offensive.

Talking about markets is also a poor choice of framing, because it automatically cedes ground to the right, who use the opportunity to talk about how markets bring us freedom and grow economies. Agitating against wealth or property is an improvement, but discussion about ownership also involves questions of agency; and the agency of ownership is nearly always used more effectively when pooled collectively – whereas the freedom of markets tends toward individualism.

Whilst challenging the reach of markets has been an important part of leftist thinking for a long time, historically the battlegrounds of ownership, property and property rights have been far more central to egalitarian politics. From Marx's call for workers to own the means of production, to the nineteenth century co-operative movement and back to the ancient rights of the commons, the longer-term goal of people striving for a more equal society was less about how goods and services were traded and more about who owned what and by what justification.

One crucial stage in this political struggle was the ending of slavery – the idea that one man could own another. Its defeat in the nineteenth century was an essential part of the development of a liberal politics that put individual rights – and, crucially, individual property rights – at the heart of the challenge to the feudal order. In this way, the cause of free markets emerged alongside the idea of free people: no longer slaves to be traded or indentured to a feudal lord. The liberal proponents of the new system extolled the comparative freedom of the 'free market' over the oppressive systems of ownership in feudal and slave economies. Yet new forms of injustice soon emerged: on the one hand, wage slavery; on the other, vast inequalities of wealth. These were not so much problems with markets – which are simply mechanisms for exchange – as problems with fetishising private ownership. After all, in a free market system based on private property ownership, investment and its returns as profit will continually reap the benefits of the productive economy. To put this another way, 'unregulated markets tend towards monopoly'.[2]

This has long been recognised even in the most liberal western countries. A body of competition law has grown up to check corporate concentrations of ownership – though, as the example of News International shows, it is easily circumvented. Other mechanisms, such as progressive income and wealth taxes, social security, financial and labour market regulation have, in different ways, prevented the worst excesses of a concentration of private wealth.

Yet the deregulation of the financial services sector since the 1980s in the UK (and elsewhere) has shown how quickly we can succumb to this fundamental flaw in the concatenation of markets and private property. In the UK, we have seen inequality sky-rocket, and the proportion of national income derived from wages fall from 65 per cent in 1974 to 53 per cent in 2009.[3] This statistic is compounded by massive wage inflation at the very top: a 49 per cent increase in the 2011 pay of FTSE-100 directors, while real wages for the vast majority of us fell once inflation has been taken into account.[4] What this means is that a property-owning and executive elite reap the benefit of the work the rest of us do. Research has consistently shown that this growing inequality makes our society less happy, less healthy and less cohesive.[5]

Alienation and the money managers

Perhaps shareholding offers one means of tackling the concentration of ownership? After all, most of our major corporations are publically limited companies: few are owned outright by individuals or families. This means some working people own shares in companies listed on the stock exchange, and thus a material stake in our collective prosperity. But most are alienated from the actual processes of ownership that would give them agency in the running of companies and an ability to dictate how they conduct business. Indeed, not many own shares directly; instead, investment vehicles like insurance and pension funds manage shareholdings for those of us who have access to those products. These bodies operate solely and simply with one end in mind: to maximise return on investment for their clients.

The community organiser Saul Alinsky tried at the end of his life to bring about social change through shareholder activism – ordinary shareholders instructing their pension funds to demand ethical behaviour from the companies they invested in. Potentially this could have been transformative, but the idea only caught on in a limited way due to the nature of these financial arrangements. Pensions, insurance and savings schemes are sold to us as products. Few see them as a means by which they should have a say in how our society is organised.[6]

Nor is shareholding a democratic approach to social change. In the UK 56 per cent of people have savings of £500 or less, and only 12 per cent have more than £50,000.[7] On top of this, only about 40 per cent of working age people actually have private pensions, and many of these are 'unfunded'; that is, they are not based on investment but rely on the work of future employees in their organisation.[8] So not only does our current system breed inequality, it also disempowers even the minority who have some stake in the processes of corporate ownership.

The shareholder society in practice: The Big Six energy companies

The relationship between rising inequality and our ownership system is constantly on display. Take the debate in autumn 2011 about the Big Six energy companies. These effectively maintain an oligopoly, receive huge amounts of support from the state, and are the sort of companies that produce the reliable profits that make them a good investment for pension funds. In October 2011, as the story was breaking about the rise in annual profits per customer from £15 to £125, amid increasing levels of fuel poverty, Chris Huhne appeared on the BBC's *Today Show* to talk about the action the government was taking. He argued on the one hand that consumers must get a better deal, but on the other that it was important that these companies make 'robust profits for their shareholders, because, after all, *that's us too, our pensions etc*' (emphasis added).

Except, of course, it's not 'us', it's *some* of us, and any connection some of us may have to a pension fund investment is less real and immediate than a massive electricity bill arriving on our doorstep. This invocation of some sort of 'shareholder society', where we are all invested in the profitability of companies, becomes little more than a clarion call to inaction on inequality. The rising tariffs of the big energy companies are effectively another way of channelling income from the poorer segments of our society to the richer ones. Democratic ownership of corporations through shareholdings is largely a mirage: it is mainly a way of maintaining support for the current system, which excessively benefits those who already have the most. Economist L. Randall Wray has called this model of ownership 'money manager capitalism', and he argues that it was at the root of the current economic crisis.[9]

The generational character of the crisis in ownership: housing

The cut-price sell-off of state utilities during the 1980s was portrayed as a way of democratising the benefits of economic deregulation. But more fundamental to the Thatcher government's project of building a neoliberal 'property-owning democracy' was the right-to-buy scheme for selling off council housing. In theory, this enabled many more to own their own house – and thus, through ownership of a major asset which seemed only ever to increase in value, ensured they were invested in the new order of things through a steady increase in their nominal wealth. In this way, we bought into neoliberal priorities – not so much by accepting a market in social housing but by eagerly taking the bait of private property ownership.

As a political strategy the sale of council houses was tremendously successful in convincing a whole generation that their interests aligned with the wealthiest in society. As a macroeconomic strategy, it worked fine until the property bubble burst. But the impact of right-to-buy on social mobility and generational inequality? Disastrous. As governments protect the investment of the right-to-buy generation by keeping housing prices inflated, another generation sees home ownership as an unattainable myth. In *Jilted Generation*, Ed Howker and Shiv Malik describe the situation in which this has left UK housing policy:

In Britain today, it's beyond doubt that we are getting it wrong; that the housing we build is unsuitable and the way we divide housing between us unreasonable. It's beyond doubt that we're making it more difficult for people to find housing that is permanent. We're placing insurmountable barriers in the way of success of young people, those who will fashion our society and reproduce the next generation to live in it.[10]

Housing in the UK plays into the worst excesses of our system of ownership, but working in a different way from our relationship to corporate shares. Far from being alienated from the houses we own, we are individually, culturally and economically overinvested in private housing.

While disparities in shareholding are masked by a language of democratic ownership through pensions and insurance, housing is increasingly obviously an area divided into haves and have nots. Yet owning your own home became foundational to our view of economic prosperity. This obsession, tying into our worst tendencies as human beings to compete over status, underpins our whole culture of aspiration. It means that what should be a basic necessity – a roof over our heads – becomes a form of distinction and the primary cultural indicator of financial stability.

In London, the situation has become obscene, and I experience it firsthand. As a university lecturer earning well above the national average, and assuming a generous 4-times multiplier on my salary for a possible mortgage, it would take me twenty-two years of saving a fifth of my net income to have enough for a deposit on a one bed flat in the (hardly affluent) area of London that I live in. In the meantime, I'm paying out nearly half my salary on rent and bills, mostly to a landlord who can simply sit back and reap a steady income from the shared flat I live in without lifting a finger. The only people I know under the age of 35 (outside of city workers) who have bought their own homes have received help from generous and wealthy parents. Private home ownership is not aspirational under these circumstances: it's dynastic.

London may be a exaggerated caricature of the situation in the rest of the country. But it seems that across the UK the only sector of the housing market as a whole which is booming is buy-to-let. While first-time buying dwindles, buy-to-let mortgages increased by 16 per cent between June and November 2011.[11] This is ownership concentration writ large on our towns and cities. The new purchases being made do not represent the next generation of people settling down and having kids in their shiny new homes; they are a sign of the wealthy further increasing their wealth without work, subsidised by working people.

Conclusion

Reading this far, one may be forgiven for thinking I am advocating an end to private property. Not so. Our right to own things for ourselves is fundamental. But what I am suggesting is that there should be *limits* on what we can own, and that for many things – especially housing, health, and education – collective forms of ownership are not only politically and socially desirable, but can produce better economic outcomes for the vast majority of people. This is not a one-size-fits-all call for state ownership, but instead the suggestion that if we think imaginatively about ways of owning things in common, people will find that they have more power over their lives and livelihoods.

A lot of this thinking is happening already. Shared ownership housing schemes are increasing across the UK, the John Lewis partnership is flourishing and the Co-operative Group has ambitiously set itself a target to increase its membership from 6 million to 20 million people by the end of the decade. Concepts like 'collaborative consumption' and 'co-opportunity' seek to describe ways in which people are inventively (often using digital technologies) finding ways to share the things we own, from cars to tools to local currencies.[12]

None of these models are perfect, but they are far better than what is currently dominant. If we can learn one thing from the right's success over the last thirty years it is that we need to be ready with a programme of ideas for every sector and every eventuality. Following Naomi Klein (and Milton Friedman), the 'shock doctrine' holds that when a crisis hits, policy-makers reach for the nearest solution to hand.[13] For three decades this has been to take things out of common ownership and into private ownership. For the left to mimic that success, however, this means not simply disseminating *ideas* about different models of ownership. We need to actually be practising them – otherwise we will have no experience from which to draw upon.

Ben Little is a lecturer in media and cultural studies at Middlesex University. He writes about politics, protest and popular culture and edited *Radical Future* (2010), the forerunner to *Regeneration* and the first in the Radical Future series.

Notes

1. By 2002, the richest 1 per cent of Britons were estimated to own 23 per cent of national wealth: see Office of National Statistics, Social Trends no.40, 2010, chapter 5 (Income & Wealth), p62. In the US, the richest 1 per cent own around 35 per cent of national wealth: see Robert Frank, 'Top 1 per cent Increased Their Share of Wealth in Financial Crisis', *Wall Street Journal*, 30 April 2010: http://blogs.wsj.com/wealth/2010/04/30/top-1-increased-their-share-of-wealth-in-financial-crisis/.
2. Peter Kellner, *New Mutualism: The Third Way*, The Co-op Party 1998, p5.
3. Stewart Lansley, *Unfair to Middling: How Middle Income Britain's shrinking wages fuelled the crash and threaten recovery*, TUC 2009, p4.
4. Anonymous, 'Directors' pay rose 50 per cent in past year, says IDS report', *BBC News Website*: www.bbc.co.uk/news/business-15487866, 28 October 2011.
5. See Richard Wilkinson and Kate Picket, *The Spirit Level*, Penguin 2009.
6. Though ethical investment funds are an expanding area of financial services, they will never tackle the root causes of these problems, which are structural.
7. Anonymous, 'More than a fifth of Britons have no savings', *The Telegraph*, 1 April 2010.

8. The figures are: 37 per cent of women and 40 per cent of men have a non-state pension as of 2005/6. Anonymous, 'Private Pensions', *Pensions Policy Institute* 2010: https://www.pensionspolicyinstitute.org.uk/default.asp?p=81.

9. L. Randall Wray, 'Money manager capitalism and the global financial crisis', *Soundings* 45, Lawrence and Wishart 2011.

10. Ed Howker and Shiv Malik, *Jilted Generation*, Icon Books 2010, p65.

11. Becky Barrow, 'Buy-to-let boom as number of loans surges 16 per cent in three months', *Daily Mail*, 10 November 2011: www.dailymail.co.uk/news/article-2059995/Buy-let-boom-number-loans-surges-16-months.html.

12. See Rachel Botsman and Roo Rogers, *What's Mine is Yours: The Rise of Collaborative Consumption*, Harper Business 2010; and John Grant, *Co-Opportunity*, Wiley 2010.

13. Naomi Klein, *The Shock Doctrine*, Penguin 2008.

The case for a new economics

Charlie Young and Rina Kuusipalo

As the final arbiter of modern politics, mainstream economics is the principal inhibitor of action on the issues we care about. Climate change, global poverty, unemployment, financial crises, debt, the break down of community – each has produced its own protest movement campaigning for incremental change. But these problems are connected systemically. If we strip away the pith, it's very difficult to come to any conclusion other than the expansive, linear nature of our economic system being at the root of our predicament.

It's time we came together to address the system. We need a new vision: a more inclusive, democratic, and realistic economic paradigm for our generation, one that puts people and planet above profit.

Modern economics is commonly defined as *the practice of distributing finite resources for the fulfilment of infinite demand.* If we are to deconstruct the old to build the new, this seems a good place to start.

Recognising ecological and social limits

If conventional economics recognises these 'finite resources', it is only as fire ants recognise the flesh of a fallen animal as finite – to be stripped and consumed with little concept of what comes when we are left with bones, other than move on. We're adept as a species at proving the finite nature of our planet. In addition to the potential catastrophe of climate change, 90 per cent of the world's old growth forests and big fish are gone, 60 per cent of the world's ecosystems are currently degraded or overused, and we are exceeding three of the earth's nine planetary boundaries.[1] When Herman Daly, then

Senior Environmental Economist at the World Bank, suggested a circle labelled 'the environment' be incorporated into a diagram of inputs and outputs of the economy, the Bank's response was to omit the diagram altogether.[2]

If we could conquer a new planet to grow on, it would be a different story. But even UK consumption is beyond its means, only possible as a result of extraterritorial expansion relentlessly extracting resources from the global South.[3] As the chasm between economics and the physical world widens, many put their hopes in technological progress, but there are physical limits to our technological efficiency. Even the celebrated Green Revolution in agriculture was temporary: our ability to increase food production per acre has levelled off since the early 2000s.[4]

Renewables and zero-carbon energy will be essential to combating climate change – yet their capacity is not infinite. To create a global infrastructure to meet today's energy demands is one challenge, but to meet the demand of a doubled population and a doubled economic growth requiring doubled energy demand? Even the former becomes dubious when we account for the massive embedded energy costs of new infrastructure and technologies, let alone the unrealistic 130-fold increase in carbon efficiency needed to reduce emissions 80 per cent by 2050 whilst maintaining growth.[5] Looking at the issue from a systemic point of view, it is clear that getting real about climate change means *reducing* production and consumption, operating on the plane of *sufficiency* rather than excess: universal wellbeing rather than decadence and poverty. To put real 'limits' on the economy, to recognise Nature, is antithetical to the ideology of unlimited growth. Accepting there are limits to the *rate* of extraction is, though obvious, a revolutionary step.

Infinite demand and social psychology

The assumption that demand is infinite, that growth is inconsequentially good, means we should consume as much as possible. But *is* demand infinite? Does sufficiency exist? More than half of Fortune 500 CEOs admit that advertising results in people buying things they don't want and don't need, and through a process of creative destruction, the 'new' often plans its obsolescence – breaking on a particular date or being superseded by the next brand wave.[6] Manufactured demand is, of course, necessary for economic growth. The breakdown of community, status competition and widening global and national inequality have rent the social fabric enough to leave a hole in our sense of self. A UNICEF report has placed the UK last for child wellbeing in the industrialised world as parents, forced by long working hours, struggle to fill emotional neglect with material goods despite children wanting 'time with family and friends and "plenty to do outdoors"'.[7] And yet the social pressure to consume is so strong that, as Tim Jackson writes, '[p]eople [are] persuaded to spend money they don't have on things we don't need to create impressions that don't last on people we don't care about'.[8] This forced demand, which may even encourage people to work longer, is one of the central justifications for the pursuit of economic growth.

Justifying hegemony

Utilitarianism, the moral philosophy that underlines this paradigm, sees maximisation of 'utility' – individual 'units' of happiness – as its ultimate goal, regardless of its distribution. This inevitably leads to vast inequalities along lines of access and power. A utilitarian would say it's better that over a year (1) Karl gets 10,000 points and Adam loses 2,000 points than if (2) both Karl and Adam get 3,500 points each –because the total number of points in (1) is greater. Similarly, the 1 per cent gaining billions can counteract the losses of the 99 per cent. We're reminded of this in the Adam Smith quote on every one of our £20 notes; growth in quantity, rather than fairer distribution, is the central tenet of policy.[9]

Loose justifications of inequality assume a growing average affluence, but the planet can't withstand increased ecological pressures from amplified consumption, production and lifestyle. In the UK as well as globally, we are living in an age of renewed inequality. London is the developed world's most unequal city with the richest tenth possessing 273 times the wealth of the poorest tenth, figures resembling those of Victorian times.[10] When we accept there are physical limits to the system – that not everybody can be rich – the myth of universal affluence, the primary pacifier of class conflict, dissolves. No wonder then that the London riots last August featured looting of shops. With almost half of London's children still living below the poverty line, looting becomes the only option to realise this illusory promise.

Internationally, the extent to which the affluence of some is built upon the exploitation of others is often understated. The developing world should be granted more space to grow to reach a sufficient level of wellbeing and developed countries need to make space: an American will have consumed, by 4am on 2 January of any given year, the same amount of resources as a Tanzanian in an entire year. Since the 1970s, global 'trickle down' of wealth has proved itself a false solution, with most developing countries plummeting into even worse poverty and inequality growing in two thirds of the world's countries.

Meanwhile, the distance over which our economic activity can now stretch is global – making it impossible to see the full effects of the consumption 'choices' we make every day. It was Keynes's advice to 'let goods be homespun whenever it is reasonably and conveniently possible'. Localism, or more accurately regionalism, can be both more efficient in ecological terms and make truly participatory democracy possible, as the effects of our actions materialise within our moral community. Some goods need to be traded internationally, like certain ores or food surplus in times of crisis, but we undeniably need to get back within our means. Regionalising puts the true carrying capacity of the earth into perspective – how much it takes to support human populations – while drawing us closer to one another and nature in a web of mutual and dynamic interdependence.

The labyrinth of finance and debt

Unregulated, unaccountable, and undemocratic, the financial system has been designed and implemented by a small minority of wealthy financial industry middlemen, who come up with products – derivatives being just one modern example – for their own gain, at the expense of the rest of humanity. Short-termist and virtually amoral, finance's golden compass is return on investment – maximising GDP. Deforesting an area, selling the timber and buying more land with the profit is evidently more productive than setting the land aside or restoration. Finance determines what grows and what stagnates and profit is the conductor of the orchestra.

Finance is built on a huge debt-driven framework, contributing to the instability of the financial system while necessitating (as a result of interest) the perpetual bubble expansion of the economy while credit and debt push us to live beyond the long-term carrying capacity of the planet and give houses of cards the appearance of solid edifices. Home mortgages are essentially designed to pacify populations under a debt that would keep them retained within and tied to the economic system. This prevents revolt, no matter how revolutionary a cause.

To really get to the root of perhaps the most fundamental issue pulling the strings of all society's efforts – finance – we must confront the concepts of money and banking not as something detached from activism, but as something we can radically transform to serve the real public interest and finance the transition to a more sustainable society. We need a new framework for finance that is more diverse and plural, more stable as well as democratic, and promoting the flourishing of people. We need finance that serves its true primary function, defined by Nobel laureate Robert Merton and elaborated on by nef as: '[t]o facilitate the allocation and deployment of economic resources, both spatially and temporally, to environmentally sustainable activities that maximise long-term financial and social returns under conditions of uncertainty'. As for potential tools to build such a system, we are swimming in them: splitting up the banks, separating retail and investment banking; hard, produce-based currency created through productive loans; green investment banks; co-operative financial structures; local currencies; and localised, community banking.

Real wellbeing, progress and equilibrium

People's levels of satisfaction and happiness correlate with increasing GDP up to a certain level but after people's real needs are satisfied the relationship disintegrates fairly quickly. The percentage of Americans, for example, who said they were 'very happy with their lives' peaked in 1956 when the nation's wealth was a third of what it is now. The same is also true for individual levels of wealth. GDP, after all, is an inaccurate and brutal indicator. It measures quantity, not quality. If our water becomes too fouled for drinking and we have to buy bottled water, the purchase counts as a positive, as does the production of equipment needed to clear up an oil spill. We work longer hours than medieval peasants, and levels of trust and sense of community continue to drop as the economy expands and inequality rises.[11] By directing society toward new indicators of progress based on wellbeing and ecological resilience, we free ourselves from the insane drive of perpetually expanding production and meaningless work. We co-produce (relying more on those around us) what we need and collectively reduce our working hours to give us more time to follow our passions.

But under the current framework consuming less en masse leads to unemployment, general depression and collapse. The kinds of work we dream of – people-heavy, experience-based, hands-on activities which minimise material consumption – are, by definition, labour intensive and therefore antithetical to economic growth. At this point we must ask ourselves which is more important to humanity, a torpedo of an economy propelling itself into the great nowhere on dwindling fuel reserves or human wellbeing and ecological integrity.

The Commons and alternative ownership models

It seems rational, even to Marxists like John Bellamy Foster, that individuals and communities retain the right to own and benefit from the improvements arising as a result of their labour. What is often not discussed, however, is the supreme wealth of the global Commons making that labour possible, and who should own them.

The Romans differentiated between private (*res privatae*), public (*res publicae*), and common interests (*res communes*). The land, the sky, water, ecosystems, ores, public spaces, scientific knowledge and local customs all sprang from nature's abundance and the life's work of previous generations. Today, these Commons are mostly held in private hands and when traded for profit, their consumption and degradation are maximised rather than their conservation and reverence as the fragile and finite foundations of all life. Centralising control of land, for example, raises prices and forces people off soil they may have farmed or inhabited for generations, rising property tax makes sustainable land use an impossible subsistence activity and uproots entire cultures. When separated from the means of subsistence we are inevitably reliant on those who control the Commons for our very survival. The state is hardly the counterpoint: each year at the UN climate talks, we see corporate (private) and nation state (public) interests trump those of the ecosphere (commons). We need a whole new set of inclusive institutions, governance property rights and monetary systems dedicated to protection and management of the Commons.

Reimagining economics

Economics may seem vastly complex and excessively corporate, but it is essential that we don't leave it to the economists. As we have argued, getting the economic system right is fundamental to everything we wish to achieve. Economics is neutral as a tool – defined politically by those dominating its use – but just as money is not bad in itself, essentially a token for exchange between humans, economics is not inherently evil.

When things that make rational, emotional, and practical sense – like ending poverty, building community and protecting the environment – fail to make economic sense, it simply means that our economics no longer makes sense. Economics should be a possibility for all, and it is time we take back control of what is ours and harness the immense power we collectively possess to inspire and organise around what could be the graceful transition of humanity into a new era of stewardship and equilibrium.

There might be necessity in the natural world; but outside the crumbling human constructs, there is nothing but urgent possibility, to be imagined, and enacted, by us.

Charlie Young has worked for and volunteered for more than fifteen think tanks, NGOs and governments from the US and UK to Uganda, Mexico, Costa Rica and Kiribati, including the New Economics Foundation, 350.org, the Labour and Green parties in the House of Commons, 10:10 and the Welsh Assembly. He has been awarded UK youth activist of the year and elected to represent his generation at the World Economic Forum, G20 and Global Humanitarian Forum. He is currently studying at Harvard University, and co-founding a progressive New Economics youth think tank, working extensively with the New Economics Institute; he is also helping coordinate a series of initiatives to integrate new economics into the youth movement for the Rio+20 Earth Summit.

Rina Kuusipalo is a student at Harvard concentrating in Social

Studies, and co-founder of Organizing for a New Economy. She has been involved in Occupy Boston and Occupy Harvard; is the Secretary and Policy Director of Harvard's Environmental Action Committee; a part-time intern at Alternatives for Community; and, as a SustainUS youth delegate, has attended and drafted policy for UN-CSocD, UN-CSD, as well as the upcoming COP 17 climate negotiations and the Rio+20 Earth Summit.

Notes

1. Lierre Keith, Aric McBay & Derrick Jensen, *Deep Green Resistance: Strategy to Save the Planet*, 2010; *Millennium Ecosystems Assessment*: maweb.org/en/index.aspx, 2005;
   Rockstrom et al, 'Planetary Boundaries: Exploring the Safe Operating Space for Humanity', *Ecology and Society* 14(2): 32, 2009.
2. Herman Daly, *Beyond Growth*, 1996.
3. The UK's greenhouse gas emissions continue to rise on a consumption basis – we are outsourcing the costs of cleanup to countries like China and benefiting from their carbon sinks. See, for example, Carbon Trust, *International Carbon Flows research*, May 2011.
4. Mario Giampietro, 'Multi-scale integrated analysis of agro-ecosystems', CRC Press 2004; see Norman Borlaug's Nobel Prize speech, 1970.
5. Tim Jackson, *Prosperity Without Growth*, Routledge 2009.
6. Serge Latouche, *Petit traité de la décroissance sereine*, Mille et une Nuits 2007.
7. Randeep Ramesh, 'UK children stuck in "materialistic trap"', *The Guardian*, 13.9.11: guardian.co.uk/society/2011/sep/14/uk-children-stuck-materialistic-trap.
8. *Prosperity Without Growth*, op. cit.
9. In case you haven't got a £20 note to hand, the Adam Smith quote on it reads: 'The division of labour in pin manufacturing (and the great increase in the quantity of work that results) ...'
10. Daniel Dorling, *Injustice:Why Social Inequality Persists*, Policy Press 2010.
11. Andrew Simms and David Boyle, *The New Economics*, Taylor Francis 2009, Chapter Six; Richard Wilkinson & Kate Pickett, *The Spirit Level:Why More Equal Societies Almost Always Do Better*, Allen Lane 2009.

Environmentalism as if climate change didn't matter

Richard George

In the dog days of 2008, the UK government passed the Climate Change Act.[1] It was the high point of political interest and awareness of climate issues; the first time any country had unilaterally committed to scientifically determined cuts in greenhouse gas emissions. Climate change had seized the public imagination in a big way; few public figures could resist the low-carbon bandwagon. In a breathtakingly confused moment that perfectly captured the mood, *Vogue* magazine chose to fly Leonardo diCaprio to Iceland to pose for the front page of its 'green issue'.[2] Even the Conservative Party, in the process of detoxifying its brand, changed its logo to a tree and sent its leader to the Arctic to pose with a pack of huskies.

The Climate Change Act was meant to inspire an arms race of similar deals, climaxing in a new global deal at the 2009 climate change talks in Copenhagen. There was a very real sense that something massive was about to happen. 'In every era there are only one or two moments when nations come together and ... make history,' announced then prime minister Gordon Brown, who was renowned for not taking climate change seriously. 'Copenhagen must be such a time. For the planet there is no Plan B'.[3]

By the end of 2009 it was all over. The climate deal had been abandoned; Gordon Brown, who'd travelled to the conference a couple of days early to try and secure his place in history, wasn't even allowed into the room where the real decisions were being made. The international consensus over tackling climate change and moving towards a low-carbon economy had been jettisoned. In its place was a forcefully compelling narrative, brought about by the global recession, which placed economic growth above all else. Those first tentative steps towards living within our ecological means had been brought to a miserable halt as the economists remade the world in their idealised, ideological image.

Some tried to fight it. There was lofty talk of a 'green new deal': twenty-first century Keynesianism built around a low-carbon economy.[4] Climate activists began engaging proactively in workers' issues, talking about a 'just transition' to a more equitable economy built on wind farms and electric cars.[5] One report went even further, arguing that Britain could and should go zero-carbon, trumping the 80 per cent cut in CO2 emissions that ministers had already agreed to.[6] Many of us welcomed the chance for some systemic critique: to highlight the links between capital and carbon. But for all our good intentions, talk of 'steady state' economics and sustainable economies just sounded hollow and naïve while the Bank of England was slashing interest rates and thousands were tearfully clearing out their desks.

We kept at it though, and for a brief moment in April 2009 it looked like we'd done the impossible: woven our red and green threads into a radically progressive tapestry. As the G20 descended on London to work out how much of our money the wealth creators needed to stay afloat, hordes of people converged on the Bank of England and the Carbon Exchange in simultaneous protests against the corporate takeover of both climate change and capital.[7] But six months later, when Copenhagen collapsed in a sea of corporate lobbying and backroom deals, it had become all too clear that global politics had no interest in being reminded about its carbon footprint. There was a recession on, after all.

What really strikes me when I look back with the glorious clarity of hindsight is that the ideas were pretty sensible, but the narrative totally sucked. It's not like cutting consumption is a luxury: even if we leave the carbon aside, no amount of wishful thinking will stop us running out of oil, copper and the fancy metals that power our mobile phones.[8] But with stock markets crashing and a new and exciting financial lexicon for the media to get its head around, there just wasn't any space for abstract problems like climate change or ecological footprints. Becoming increasingly shrill, as many panic-stricken commentators chose to do, just made the problem worse. You can't talk about '100 months to save the world' when everyone else is only interested in the economy and keeping food on the table.

But enough navel-gazing: how can we get things back on track and kick-start climate movement 2.0?

At the risk of being overly divisive, I'd question whether we want to. Is climate change the most important issue for us to campaign on at the moment? All around us, national institutions that we once thought unassailable are being dismantled at an alarming rate. Sure, that's happened before, but under the Conservative-Liberal Democrat coalition it's happening apace and exceptionally publicly. Most people only have a limited amount of time to campaign; can we justify dragging them away from saving their local library or stopping the carve-up of the National Health Service? Even self-defined climate activists have jobs, families and lives to live outside of the activist bubble. We're all involved in other campaigns (and if we aren't, we should be); is there a compelling reason to make climate change our favourite cause at the expense of other issues? Besides, if climate change is a systemic problem, might we be better off putting overt environmentalism aside for a year or two and helping build a constituency that challenges the system, not the symptoms?

I'm not proposing that we leave the climate to fend for itself. But we need to recognise that the politics has changed and change our rhetoric accordingly. Thankfully, most of what we're arguing for doesn't just make sense on ecological grounds: at a macro level there are rock-solid social and economic arguments too. The real difference should be in our micro-level solutions and our presentation. Look at the sectors where carbon emissions are most intransigent: energy and transport. The macro solution is to use less fuel. But for the last decade mainstream environmentalists have argued for market-based solutions: pricing scarce resources so that people were forced to drive less or turn their televisions off at the wall. That's not going to work in a recession when regulations of all kinds are rebranded as 'job killers'.[9] The last government might have been prepared to introduce unpopular restrictions on people's freedom in the public interest; this one certainly isn't going to (at least, not for any of the causes we care about).

Besides, no government on earth would be so stupid as to price petrol and electricity so that it actually forces people to change their behaviour. Using pricing and markets to stop climate change forces us into pitched battles over 1p increases in fuel duty. It makes us waste our time trying to monetise the damage caused by emitting one tonne of carbon dioxide. Not only does that not get us what we want, it allows our opponents to paint us as uncaring, authoritarian and out of touch with ordinary people.

So what's the best angle, the best way to approach the underlying structural problems which plague our societies? We could start by recognising that the companies and individuals who are standing in the way of climate progress are the same companies which are screwing us economically. It's also time we stopped trying to turn everyone into activists.[10] More activism, with all the connotations that loaded word contains, isn't an objective, but one potential means to an end.[11] We can achieve our goals without forcing everyone to attend direct action camps or organise by consensus, even if we find those tools helpful to our own organising. Then we need to accept that it wasn't a lack of systemic critique that got us where we are. There were plenty of attempts to identify capitalism as the root cause of climate disaster: that's why business was so determined to lobby the Copenhagen climate talks.[12]

Less palatably, I think that we have to question whether there is any point in campaigning in environmental terms if people aren't receptive to that line of argument. Instead, shouldn't we be looking for the most strategic way to advance our vision of a more progressive and sustainable society? The climate frame certainly used to be the best way to advance our vision, but it isn't at the moment. Most people can't do much to stop climate change on their own, especially when government and business is determinedly retrograde. Focusing on climate for its own sake, and individual actions as the solution, can make people feel disempowered. It's no good asking people to drive fewer miles if we don't start designing environments that make it easy for people to walk and cycle. No one wants to sit in traffic for an hour to get to work, but they'll do so if the alternative is going without food. If you give up flying, but none of your friends do, you don't feel like you're having an impact, you just feel left out.

So instead of talking about loft lagging and nudges, let's focus our attention on the real villains. The banks are a tempting target, but corporate finance of carbon-intensive industries is too abstract to go mainstream. I'd look at the politics of energy instead. The Big Six energy companies have hiked fuel bills by almost 20 per cent, using environmental taxes as a convenient smokescreen.[13] In practice, green taxes are just 4 per cent of gas bills (10 per cent of electricity bills), and they're funding efficiency measures which should save households money in the short, medium and long term.[14] We should be making common cause with fuel poverty groups, but the prevailing narrative sets us against each other. Not only do we not need to base those arguments on ecological grounds, but we're better off dropping the climate rhetoric and talking – ironically, just as David Cameron once did – about quality of life. This is a golden opportunity to turn using less energy into a big 'fuck you' to these corporate profiteers, not some hair-shirt response to an intangible global crisis.

This approach isn't without its downsides. Climate change, unlike world peace or child poverty, has a deadline. The warming effect of carbon dioxide emissions continue for some time, so every tonne we can stop emitting now is worth more than one abated in a decade or two. We also run the risk of further entrenching high carbon behaviour, which will make it harder to effect the change we need. But if we aren't careful we risk alienating people and allowing the insidious 'growth at all costs' agenda to cement its hold. If – and I accept that it's a big if – we can use social and economic messages to challenge carbon intensive behaviour, then we stand a chance of stopping the feral elite from trashing society and our climate. If the alternative is economic, social and environmental disaster, I don't think we have any other options.

Tackling climate change will take more than a few regulations and an eco-tax or two, and there's no political appetite for either. It's going to take some structural changes that will hurt the few but benefit the rest. Put in those terms, the debate necessarily becomes one of values, not parts-per-million and carbon pricing. That's the really important battle: only by winning the argument about who and what is valuable to our society do we stand any hope of sorting climate change out. If we can't make the case for a society built on equity, then what hope do we have for taking on the forces of economic growth? It's time to stop talking about saving society from climate change and start talking about the sort of society we want to save. Don't worry – saving the world will still be here when we get back.

Richard George has been involved with grassroots environmental activism for much of the past decade. He was a founding member of Plane Stupid, which took direct action against the government's plans for airport expansion. Richard now works for Greenpeace as a climate campaigner and harbours a not-so-secret desire to study Victorian anti-enclosure protests.

Notes

1. *Climate Change Act 2008*, HMSO 2008: www.legislation.gov.uk/ukpga/2008/27.
2. Environment Issue, *Vanity Fair*, 2007.
3. Alison Chung, 'PM Warns "There Is No Plan B" For The Planet', *Sky News* 2009: http://news.sky.com/home/politics/article/15408565.

4. *The Green New Deal*, New Economics Foundation 2008: www.neweconomics.org/projects/green-new-deal.

5. Jonathan Neale (ed.), *One Million Climate Jobs*, Campaign Against Climate Change 2010, www.campaigncc.org/greenjobs.

6. Martin Kemp (ed.), *Zero Carbon Britain 2030: a new energy strategy*, Centre for Alternative Technology 2007.

7. Dominic Casciani , 'Eyewitness: Climate Camp in the City', *BBC News*, 2009, http://news.bbc.co.uk/1/hi/uk/7977863.stm.

8. See, for instance, Jean Laherrère, 'Amazing Presentation On The End Of The Copper Era', *Business Insider*, 2010: www.businessinsider.com/peak-copper-2010-4.

9. This rhetoric is not as widespread in the UK as in the United States, but its influence on policy can be seen in the UK government's Red Tape Challenge programme, which attempted to 'crowd source' everything from health and safety regulation to legislation governing rare species, rights of way and fluorine gas.

10. 'Give up activism', *Do or Die*, issue 9, pp160-6, 1999: www.eco-action.org/dod/no9/activism.htm.

11. Liza Featherstone, Doug Henwood and Christian Parenti, '"Action Will Be Taken": Left Anti-intellectualism and Its Discontents', *Radical Society*, 2002: www.leftbusinessobserver.com/Action.html.

12. Kate Willson and Andrew Green, 'The Business Lobby in Copenhagen', *Huffington Post*, 2010: www.huffingtonpost.com/2009/12/18/the-business-lobby-in-cop_n_397128.html.

13. Michael Kavanagh and Sylvia Pfeifer, 'Calls for simpler tariffs as "big six" profits soar', *Financial Times*, 2011: www.ft.com/cms/s/0/b95580f8-f63a-11e0-824e-0144feab49a.

14. *Updated Household energy bills explained*, Ofgem 2011: www.ofgem.gov.uk/Media/FactSheets/Documents1/updatedhouseholdbillsjan11.pdf. Wholesale energy prices and companies profit margins make up 63 per cent of electricity, and 64 per cent of gas bills.

The feminist evolution: queer feminism for the next generation

Ray Filar

Feminism must evolve or it will stagnate. The institutional discriminations British women face today may still, in many ways, be the same they were forty years ago, but the solutions won't and can't be. Pick up a copy of Germaine Greer's *The Female Eunuch*, first published in 1970. The continuing relevance of her analysis is staggering. Life for women has changed only somewhat –nominal legislative equality is, arguably, the biggest step forward that British feminism has enabled – but society in general has changed almost entirely. If feminism as a movement cannot adjust to keep pace, we cannot expect to keep creating change as we have done so far.

Today's feminists are indebted to the women and men of the past who fought tooth and nail to drive through what legal and political progress we have seen in the last hundred years. It can't stop there. A static feminism with ideas that stop at the new millennium is a feminism that clutches her side, gasping for air, as ever-bolstered patriarchy bounds into the distance.

It is time for feminists to take on some fresh concepts – and that means really opening our eyes to queer ideas. We need to think about the fluidity of gender, about 'genderqueer' identities – what does it mean to identify as neither male nor female, or both, or either at different times? What can we learn from trans politics, from people who also suffer gender exclusion, who also question what it means to assign gender? How do these approaches to gender affect the collective political organisation of the oppressed class of people marked 'women'? We need to talk about sexualities, about femininity and masculinity as potential sources of affirmation when conceived of separately from the socially gendered bodies of women and men. Continuing the work of 'second wave' feminists from the 1960s, we need to create alternative kinship models to supplement and question the nuclear family.[1] Evolving feminism combines multiple feminist ideologies with conceptions of how these apply to real life. As society changes, feminism must too.

Old problems/new problems

Though the time has come for the recognition that new feminist solutions are needed, *few of the issues identified by past feminist pioneers have really gone away.* Women are still over-represented in the lowest paid jobs, and under-represented in the highest, not to mention the unpaid labour women still disproportionately perform as primary child carers. We still own less property, and we hold many, many fewer positions of political power. Women of colour, women with disabilities, trans women and older women are still rendered politically invisible though sexism's insidious combination with additional forms of oppression. Two women in the UK are killed by their partners every week,[2] whilst the rape conviction rate languishes pathetically at six per cent.[3] At the same time, rape crisis centres close due to lack of funding, and the mythology that women lie about rape is perpetrated by the national press. Is it surprising that one in four women who are raped or sexually assaulted are reluctant to go to the police?[4]

These same old problems have now been joined by some new ones. 2011 saw the start of the Coalition government's attack on public services, which disproportionately affect women as users and employees. Concurrently, the public sphere of paid labour becomes precarious; as temping agencies proliferate, jobs are increasingly instable and insecure. Women make up the majority of the 'precariat' – low-paid 'flexible' workers with few rights.[5] A renewed assault on reproductive rights is under way, and with anti-choice MPs clogging up parliament's back benches it is increasingly obvious that rights taken for granted can be rights taken away.

Meanwhile, the sexual liberation that the sexual revolution promised turned out to be a red, misogynist herring. In spite of women's attempts to expand the possibilities for our own ideas of sexuality, the male-centric traditional definition of sex creates and is then reinforced by the most popular pages on the internet – those which, overwhelmingly created by men, eroticise female sexual submission and male dominance in a narrow, limiting style. This kind of pornography expresses power dynamics in sex almost entirely through the lens of misogyny and racism. This is troubling whatever kind of sex you're interested in, whatever attitude you take towards pornography as a concept: neither vanilla nor kinky sex should be centred around expressions of misogyny towards submissive partners, nor the identification of submissiveness with femaleness.

The feminist resurgence?

It's clear that the tired valuation 'men>women' will continue to hover implicitly below the surface of our cultural consciousness until it is repeatedly taken out, exposed, challenged and changed. Yet much has been made of a 'feminist resurgence' over the last few years. Breathless, hopeful media features hail each culturally recognised feminist moment as a never-before-seen-or-conceived-of breakthrough heralding a new 'wave' of activism. One notable *Evening Standard* article of 2011 hailed the 'March of the new feminists', apparently represented by four (admirable) white women positioned like groupies behind one white man.[6] I have a huge amount of respect for and interest in the ideas of anyone working in feminist writing, politics or activism right now, but let's acquire some perspective. The fourth, fifth, or whatever wave we're on now can't be started in order to sell copy.

It has been argued that before the feminist resurgence, during the so-called 'post-feminist' era of the late 1990s and early 2000s, capitalism successfully co-opted the rhetoric of women's liberation in order to sell products,[7] whilst throwing aside the word 'feminist' as connoting a kind of lesbianism that selfishly ignores male participation. It's great that mainstream culture has decided that feminism can sometimes be marketed as 'cool' and 'new' again, but it doesn't take a genius to see that feminists hadn't simply gone off for an extended beach break during those wilderness years. There's some truth in the idea of a resurgence – the recent spate of popular feminist books is testament to it – but not because feminism ever stopped. It's just that back then no-one was listening.[8] Now feminism has a small window of opportunity through which to sidle up to the public ear and make it listen. Let's not waste it.

A new evolution in feminist thought

Change is happening in a new direction; we need to get on board. It's a change that makes sense. I'm interested in a small movement that's developing, 'queer feminism'. The theoretical bit of queer, known in universities as 'queer theory', has its roots firmly in feminist thought. Ideas like polyamory, for example, in which a person may proudly have many romantic partners at the same time, are entirely consistent with Andrea Dworkin's criticisms of sexual intercourse as possession or ownership.[9] Polyamory opens the door for the alternative forms of family that past radical and marxist feminists identified as potentialities for women's liberation. If heterosexual monogamy were no longer assumed to be the given, natural orientation, people of all or any genders could relate to each other in previously stigmatised ways. It doesn't take much to envisage the consequences of this for women's bodily, sexual and reproductive autonomy.

Unlike most branches of thought, many of queer theory's classic texts are written by 'women': Judith Butler, Eve Kosofsky Sedgwick,

Teresa de Lauretis, Kate Bornstein. At heart, the queer idea that gender is really fluid, that the categories 'male' and 'female' are cultural fictions which we align ourselves with through repeated gendered actions (I become a woman only because I behave like a woman), is a development of feminist writing about socialisation and the distinction between sex (sexual characteristics and chromosomes) and gender (everything else).

Queer is often characterised by deviation from the norm. To adopt a queer approach to gender is to recognise that transgression, subversion and play are kinds of anti-normative political activism that can also disrupt existing gender hierarchies. One person born with a body called 'female' assuming the trappings of masculinity is unlikely to change any government policy about women as a class, but neither was the vote won by one women chaining herself to the railings of Westminster. In time-honoured suffragette style, the more people who, by manipulating gender, expose cultural dogma about men and women for what it is – arbitrary and abusive – the more the binary line dividing 'M' from 'F' trembles.

In spite of overlap between queer and feminism, there's been some resistance to queer ideas from some feminist quarters (too elitist, too difficult to read, too 'fun', not 'radical' enough) – mixed with some worthwhile criticism of the queer movement for potentially subsuming lesbianism under a male-led and defined culture.[10] Others, however, have embraced queer as a potentially liberating force for feminists. 2011 saw a global diffusion of the 'Slutwalk' movement – reclaiming the word 'slut' and opposing sexual violence as a way to embrace women's sexual agency. It was an interesting example of how queer approaches to feminism can stimulate the public imagination. The Slutwalk message, that rape is caused only by rapists (and cannot be blamed on women drinking, wearing short skirts, etc), became integrated with the project to defuse the word 'slut' by reclaiming it. The overall message was a heavily feminist one; the underlying project was straight out of the book of queer reclamation (remember when 'queer' was a pejorative?). It was challenging, inspiring and successful. It's that same rebellious spirit that is brought out when queer subversion joins with feminist criticism to create a new kind of feminism – one that has the potential, now, to really stimulate change.

Queer feminism

Queer feminism exposes through both demonstration and argument just how incredibly silly gender generalisations are: such as, 'women biologically just don't like being CEOs', or 'men biologically can't talk about feelings'. Of course there is no intrinsic connection between labia and lip gloss; obviously the fact that women stereotypically like lip gloss has nothing to do with chromosomes and everything to do with culture. If I can be a woman today and a man tomorrow, by what logic do my genitalia at birth assign me to a category irrevocably destined for a particular kind of socialisation? Queer feminism combines the potential that choice about our gender(s) holds, with the rigorous critique of patriarchy necessary to a social justice movement. It enables freer expression of gender in the context of the wider project of ending gender injustice. It doesn't dispense with the tried and tested feminist methods of writing, campaigning, lobbying and activism – it uses them again, revitalised, to adopt new perspectives for the future of gender equality.

Queer feminism conducts a re-analysis of 'femininity' and 'masculinity' in a context that understands that femininity could just as naturally be done by men, that masculinity could just as naturally be done by women. Could femininity be powerful? What is male femininity? What does femininity mean when it isn't defined by misogyny and misogynists? Queer feminism applies the experiences of people who identify in some way outside the gender binary – as trans, as intersex, as homosexual, as gender non-conforming – to a system which mistakenly believes there are only two categories. Queer feminism opens up possibilities for sex and sexual expression – there is no right way to fuck but sex is always political. Queer feminism understands that sexism is oppressive to everyone, that it limits the way that all people live their lives.

Queer feminism, above all, is happening now. The shocking revelation that young people are just as political as previous generations goes arm in arm with this flowering movement. Queer activists are embracing queer feminism when they set up political groups which espouse feminism as intrinsic to opposing all forms of discrimination. Feminist activists do it when they create safe spaces which recognise the possibilities of queer for feminism. Lesbian, gay, bisexual and trans people are doing it when they recognise the connections between sexual orientation and gender orientation, and use that understanding to challenge gender norms and gender oppression. Young women in university feminist groups explore queer feminism when they oppose misogyny with minds influenced by queer theory and the sexual possibilities of freedom from home. Women artists play with queer feminism when they question the performance of gender on stage. Increasingly, people write about it.[11] By deconstructing gender, queer feminism exposes sexism. Queer feminism is powerful, and it is the future.

Ray Filar is a feminist blogger and freelance journalist, interested mainly in politics, gender and sexuality. She is currently a graduate student in Gender Studies at the University of Cambridge. She writes a strident feminist blog called 'Political Correctness Gone Mad'. Her work has been published in various magazines and blogs, including at *Comment is Free*, openDemocracy, *Pink News*, The F Word and Liberal Conspiracy. You can follow her twitter on @ rayfilar.

Notes

1. An exciting example of this in early queer thought is Eve Kosofsky Sedgwick's 'Tales of the Avunculate', in *Tendencies*, Duke University Press, 1993.

2. Catherine Grant, Alex Harvey, Keith Boiling and Sam Clemens, *2004–5 British Crime Survey*, 2004.
3. Ibid.
4. Home Office, *Cross Government Action Plan on Sexual Violence and Abuse*, HM Government, 2007.
5. La Eskalera Karakola, 'Precarias a la deriva: Adrift through the circuits of feminized precarious work', Traficantes de Sueños, Madrid 2004.
6. Rosamund Urwin, 'March of the new feminists', *Evening Standard*, 8 June 2011.
7. Nina Power, *One Dimensional Woman*, Zero Books 2009.
8. Some good examples: Kat Banyard, *The Equality Illusion*, Faber & Faber 2010; Catherine Redfern and Kristin Aune, *Reclaiming the F-Word*, Zed Books 2010; Natasha Walter, *Living Dolls,* Virago Press 2011.
9. Andrea Dworkin, Intercourse, Basic Books 2006 (1986).
10. Sheila Jeffreys, *Unpacking Queer Politics*, Polity Press 2002.
11. Mimi Marinucci, *Feminism Is Queer: The Intimate Connection between Queer and Feminist Theory*, Zed Books 2010.

Democracy beyond Westminster

Becky Luff

The 'No' result in May's referendum on the Alternative Vote brought great disappointment to those campaigning for change. But this does not mean we should give up on the campaign for greater democracy, both globally and locally.

The AV campaign

The disappointment of the referendum result was not only in failing to move away from the archaic voting system of First Past the Post – a system which concentrates voter power into the hands of the tiny proportion of the electorate who live in marginal seats, and turns election debate into bland politicking solely aimed at gaining the support of this 'Middle England' minority. There was also the disappointment of seeing the bursting of the bubble of enthusiasm that had surrounded democratic reform in the previous few years, bringing it into the mainstream for the first time in decades.

With a growing alienation from the Parliament that is supposed to represent them, people from varying political backgrounds had begun to see the solution in the form of institutional reform. The idea was simple: clean the mechanism by which we choose who and how politicians represent us and perhaps we'll see better decision-making, with some nuance to the debate.

The offer of a referendum – a pure form of direct democracy in which all voters have an equal say in the making of the decision – appeared to mark the success of sustained campaigning by democracy activists. Unfortunately the realpolitik proved somewhat different.

Whilst the referendum appeared in principle to offer the whole electorate the option of choosing the way they elect their MPs, the decision as to what options they would be offered had already been decided. The Alternative Vote was not the front-runner in the minds of democratic reform activists, because it fails to guarantee a proportional outcome. In addition, allowing only a yes/no option on an issue of this complexity, particularly within the media climate that surrounds Westminster, was not conducive for the true deliberative process that is needed for real direct democracy. Finally, the lack of legal regulation regarding what was said within the referendum campaign materials and advertising meant that anything could be said to support the case for either a Yes or No vote, without much concern for the truth or validity of the claims. This was a further reason for a very low level of debate.

Many activists were drawn to the democratic reform movement to improve the decision-making within Westminster politics. But, given the political road-block that the No result placed on further Parliamentary reform, perhaps it is time to look beyond Westminster, at improving the ways in which decisions are made in other forums.

Local

The level of attention and scrutiny accorded to MPs and Westminster politics, means that it is unsurprising that the role of local government is often overshadowed, particularly for those outside the political classes. And yet it is the local council that handles many of the decisions that directly affect our day-to-day lives.

This lack of attention can also be attributed to a lack of belief in the power of local government, given the limitations imposed on them by central government. People often lament the decline of community spirit and independent local business and facilities, and the rise of gentrification and chain supermarkets, but see their local government as either unwilling or powerless to do anything about it.

These were some of the concerns that drove a civil-society coalition that demanded a greater voice for local citizens that resulted in the 2007 Sustainable Communities Act.[1] This Act establishes the potential for a process by which councils, in consultation with local communities, can drive government policy on the subjects of local economies, environmental protection, social inclusion and democratic participation. Since the law was passed, one hundred councils have chosen to opt in;[2] and three hundred proposals have been made, two hundred of which were passed to relevant central government departments.[3]

Theoretically, this law could be a radical new tool for empowering local councils on behalf of their constituents. However, it requires active partnerships between citizens and their local councils to ensure that its theoretical power is actualised.

There are clear examples of local groups wishing to build stronger community links, such as Transition Towns, local anti-cuts groups, or community campaigns on the AV referendum. For these groups, and other new groups wishing to work at a local level, this new law could be an interesting way of affecting decision-making within central government.

Transnational

Many progressive activists in the UK see the European Union as an impenetrable and unaccountable trading bloc, aimed solely at furthering the cause of transnational corporations, and they react to this by choosing not to engage with European politics. But, though it is true that the origins of the European Union were based on economic unity, its early architects also saw Europe-wide political union as a necessary development. By the time the UK was accepted into the European Economic Community (as it was then called) in 1972, the European Parliament had been instituted.

The importance of having a parliament alongside a governing mechanism, at whatever level of decision-making, should not be underestimated. Unlike a government, whose primary characteristics of strength and effectiveness are driven through the streamlined unity of one voice, parliaments are designed to provide the space for discussion and debate. And throughout the evolution of the European Union, legislative power has been handed little by little from the Council of Ministers (made up of representatives from Member States' national governments) to the directly elected European Parliament. Essentially this means transfer of power from governments to a (directly elected) parliament. This is almost unheard of anywhere else in our political system.

The competition-focused EU that we have today is seen by many as problematic, but business-driven policy is not an intrinsic part of transnational integration and, like all politics, can be changed. But it must be changed from within the EU structures – it cannot be solved by piecemeal national policies. If progressive activists want to see a different EU, they should look to the way businesses have operated within the EU to learn methods of engagement. Freedom of movement (not to mention available funding from the European Commission assigned specifically for building European identity and citizenship, particularly amongst young people) could be used to build a transnational civil society network to affect change within the EU. A group already seeking to do this are the Transeuropa Network, set up by European Alternatives, to deliberate on what a European political and cultural identity would look like.

In addition – while bearing in mind the limited impact that counter-lobbying can have without the resources that businesses have at their disposal – we must also use the tools that are designed specifically to represent us: our directly elected European Parliament, elected using a proportional voting system. Unfortunately many people believe that the Parliament has little power, and therefore do not see the value in voting or holding their MEPs to account. But this precisely helps to create the democratic deficit felt so acutely by the British and others regarding their involvement with the European

Union. We rarely think about holding the transnational European parties to account. Given the increase in the Parliament's power, it seems like it may be about time we did.

Global

It has become increasingly clear that the people of the world have little or no control over global affairs. And yet there is often hesitancy about supporting proposals to strengthen the governance of global political institutions. Many see strengthening global institutions as a gateway to a world government, in which the fear is that decision-making would be consolidated to one all-powerful, unaccountable (and highly corruptible) body. Yet this is to overlook that we already have many such unaccountable bodies.

We have the G20 – an unaccountable body of financial ministers from the world's largest economies who come together once a year to set global financial strategy. We also have the United Nations Security Council, whose membership is made up of ten members, five of whom – the 'winners' of World War Two – have permanent seats. These five (the UK, US, France, Russia and China) also possess the power to veto any decision, including those that have been passed by the UN General Assembly. We also have the International Monetary Fund, the World Bank and the World Trade Organisation, powerful international bodies that come together to set global policy, with little to no accountability or internal democracy.[4]

The lack of accountability in these institutions has left us with little or no opportunity for reform. Even the bodies with representation from every nation state are explicitly designed to represent their governments, not citizens. Given the lack of representation and accountability of many governments around the world – including that of the UK – the fact that all global dialogue takes place between governments does not provide much comfort to a progressive activist wishing to see fundamental global reform.

Given this lack of representation and accountability at the global level, alongside increasing concern about economic and environmental instability, it is unsurprising that alienation with global institutions is at an all-time high, and that there are increasing calls for global democracy.

The Occupy movements (particularly of 15 October 2011) are a direct response to this alienation.[5] Once faith and patience with institutions at all levels of decision-making has been lost, the only route remaining is that of direct action aimed at reclaiming space in which to create a new democracy. The Occupy movement has shown the world that there is an alternative form of democracy – direct democracy based on consensus decision-making within inclusive People's Assemblies. Rejecting the concept of representative democracy, each person speaks for herself and herself only. Although the Assemblies are geographically local, there is much communication in order to build solidarity between Assemblies across the world.

Given the inability of the establishment to show any signs of changing 'business as usual', these alternative forms of democracy are important and must be heard. However, there seems to be a fundamental problem with the idea that this can be the one and only solution to the problems at hand. Within a People's Assembly, each individual has an equal right to representation within the process. However, what about the people who do not wish to join? What representation do they receive within the process, and how can they hold it to account, if they do not like the decisions that have been made?

An important aspect of representative democracy is that citizens gain representation automatically, whether or not they have voted or have even registered to vote. An alternative proposal for building global democracy, based on a representative democracy approach, would be to create a directly elected Parliamentary Assembly to sit within the UN. There are alternative approaches as to exactly how this would be established, but most suggest using the European

Parliament as a model, and to begin with representatives from national parliaments.[6]

The intention of a directly elected Parliament is to allow citizens to have representation at a global level, rather than states. The hope would be that the Parliamentarians would sit (and vote) according to political rather than national interests (e.g. Argentinean socialists sitting with French socialists, rather than with their fellow Argentines). Those supporting this proposal see this as the only way to bring democracy to the level needed to tackle the power of transnational corporations.[7]

One thing to bear in mind when looking to establish such a Parliamentary Assembly is that governments are not normally keen to hand over powers to parliaments. The European Parliament is an exception here, and its incremental approach may be one to be replicated. Whatever the route, it will heavily rely on pressure from civil society and leadership from under-represented citizens, if it is to have any chance of success. It will also be important at the earliest of stages to address the question of how to fund the body, to try and avoid the business-friendly relationships that are endemic in most representative democracies.

These are two quite different proposals for global democracy; but they could play complementary roles within a global democratic framework. They highlight different features of what we want from democracy, and to reject one outright in favour of another would be to limit our ambitions. Exactly what form of global democracy merges will be down to the power of the ideals, and the energy of the activists to convey them.

Conclusion

Whichever level of decision-making you are looking at, it is important to remember that democracy is an ever-evolving process, with no end point at which we can pat ourselves on the back and set off for home. Despite the failure to change the British electoral system, we cannot give up. There will be other opportunities in the future.

A common chant on protests is 'this is what democracy looks like'. What's exciting, particularly regarding the global democracy debate, but also across all levels of decision-making, is that many people have different ideas of what this democracy looks like. Fortunately, a basic tenet of democracy – whether through Parliaments or People's Assemblies – is providing the space to discuss exactly this.

Becky Luff was the East London organiser for the Yes to Fairer Votes campaign. She is the co-founder of comedy production company Lampoon Apathy, and council member for the World Federalist Movement. She currently lives in London, as part of the Big Society.

Notes

1. For information on Sustainable Communities Act 2007, see: www.localworks.org/node/5.
2. A full list of councils can be found at: http://en.wikipedia.org/wiki/List_of_local_authorities_have_opted_into_the_Sustainable_Communities_Act_2007.
3. More information on the Act at: http://en.wikipedia.org/wiki/Sustainable_Communities_Act_2007.
4. For more information on global institutions, excellent introductions can be found at http://brettonwoodsproject.org/.
5. Information about the global day of action on 15.10.11 at http://15october.net/; and http://en.wikipedia.org/wiki/October_15,_2011_protests.
6. Richard Falk and Andrew Strauss, 'Toward a Global Parliament', *The Nation*, 22.11.03: www.thirdworldtraveler.com/World_Federalism/Toward_Global_Parliament.html.
7. Campaign for the Establishment of a United Nations Parliamentary Assembly website: http://en.unpacampaign.org/about/unpa/index.php.

Reflecting on the student movement

A dialogue between Guy Aitchison and Jeremy Gilbert

Jeremy: At the risk of sounding like a grumpy middle-aged activist who's seen it all before, I want to list a number of problems with the recent anti-tuition fees campaign – but with the aim not of dismissing it but of engaging and thinking constructively about the best ways of campaigning.

Firstly, many of the claims made for the significance and originality of the campaign of were exaggerated, and often predicated on a lack of understanding of the place of the protests within recent political history. For example, one quite often heard the claim that these were the only or the most significant protests since the poll tax revolt – a very peculiar claim given that the intervening period included a wave of student occupations in 1991-2, the road protests of the early 1990s, the campaigns against the 1994 Criminal Justice Act and in support of the sacked Liverpool dockers, the anti-capitalist protests of the late 1990s and early 2000s (which was where kettling was first used as a police tactic), up to and including the radical wing of 'Make Poverty History', the European Social Forum held in London in 2004, the campaign against the Iraq invasion, etc, etc. And to claim that things like consensus decision-making and networked organisation are novel ideas is to ignore the generations of activists going back to the early 1960s who were the real pioneers of all those techniques.

The movement's discourse was couched in terms of a kind of ahistorical, unreflective boosterism – thereby exhibiting many of the key characteristics of contemporary neoliberal postmodern culture. So while the content of its discourse involved a strong critique of neoliberalism, its *form* failed to make the first, basic, most fundamental gesture of ideology-critique: namely, the accurate historicisation of its own conditions of possibility.

What's more, I would argue that the anti poll-tax campaign had no effect whatsoever on Tory government policy – which was reversed not because of the campaign but because middle-income swing voters in marginal constituencies with low property values and consequently low council rates were suddenly seeing their tax bill go up and were very unhappy about it.

Secondly, the claim that the campaign was truly socially inclusive, and not largely middle-class in character, was also dubious. Of course the participation of the 'EMA kids' was interesting and welcome (although arguably less significant than the participation of schoolchildren in the campaign against the invasion of Iraq), but the university populations that were overwhelmingly represented within the campaign were mostly very middle-class in nature, and most activity was confined to tiny rumps of middle-class students who were entirely hegemonised by the SWP, and had no grassroots support amongst the wider student population. What was problematic about all this for me was not that it was basically a middle-class campaign defending a historically middle-class privilege, but that it seemed to become impossible to acknowledge this fact, and so to start thinking about what might be done to widen and deepen the campaign's base.

Guy: Before I tackle these issues let me address some of the achievements of the movement. Though it undeniably failed in its overarching aims to stop the government lifting the cap on tuition fees and abolishing EMA, the movement did come within a whisker of defeating the Coalition government – its majority was slashed from 83 to 21, and there were three resignations. In the process, the campaign destroyed the reputation of Nick Clegg and the Liberal Democrats, exposing the hypocrisy behind their platitudes about 'fairness'. The party now regularly polls below 10 per cent, and it even lost its deposit in a by-election this year. And at the 2011 Labour Party conference, Ed Miliband's pledge to cut tuition fees by a third managed to grab the headlines. Woefully timid, for sure, but it shows what a potent issue higher education funding has become – and all without the backing of the NUS.

The other, less tangible, gain was the rise in political awareness not just amongst school and university students who discovered a sense of their own agency after years of passivity and inertia, but among all those galvanised by their stark and visible refusal to submit to the governing consensus that there is no alternative to the cuts. The Labour patrician Richard Crossman once observed with approval that Westminster is a 'rock' against which waves of popular opinion crash and break. At least we now know it's penetrable.

But how about the rhetoric? Of course it would be foolish of me to try and defend some of the more frenzied proclamations offered as instant commentary on blogs, Facebook, Twitter and the like, but I'd question the idea that students were uniquely guilty here. Take a look at 'We are Everywhere', for example, a compilation of writings from activists involved in alter-globalisation struggles, and you'll find plenty of predictions about the 'movement of movements' that seem silly today. New movements ought to be permitted some over-exuberance.

The student protest burst out of nowhere and it certainly made mistakes. And I agree too that it wasn't diverse enough – though you're perhaps too dismissive here. The presence of the EMA kids was a real phenomenon. The protests were rooted in concrete, material interests in a way that other recent protest movements have not been.

On the poll tax, the only context in which I heard it mentioned was to make the point, in the face of liberal condemnation, that antagonistic forms of protest can be a far more effective means of political contention than uniform A to B marches. I'd question your purely electoral explanation of Thatcher's defeat – with 20 million people refusing to pay, the policy simply wasn't implementable. The real tragedy was the failure to build this defiance into a mass movement. It's fundamental, I agree, to learn from the shortcomings of earlier movements and draw inspiration from their successes.

In this spirit, what do you think students can learn from the campaigns you mention? In *Anti-Capitalism and Culture* you identify the beginning of the end of the 1990s anti-roads movement with Reclaim the Streets' abandonment of an environmentalist agenda focused on Britain's countryside, in favour of the much more ambitious goal of fighting global capitalism. This move followed a well trodden path that many involved in last year's protests will recognise. How, then, do you think activists following the logic of their convictions can avoid ghettoisation?

Jeremy: I agree that some of the rhetoric at the time around the 'movement of movements' was positively millenarian in character. But this merely demonstrates that part of what I'm complaining about is in no way a new phenomenon, or even one restricted to the sphere of political activism: 20-year-olds have a tendency to imagine that they are the first and last people in history to do whatever they happen to be doing. But does this mean that the ahistoric approach and the lack of reflexivity that have characterised activist-led 'protest' movements for many years now are simply inevitable?

On the issue of the importance of organised civil disobedience in defeating the poll tax, I agree that it was important, but we have to be clear exactly what we mean here. The campaign was a factor in pressuring the government, but only because they were also vulnerable electorally. And the confrontational politics of the poll tax riots made no difference whatsoever. I had a pretty clear view of this at the time because I lived in a Tory/Lib Dem marginal constituency which the Tories lost in 1992 primarily because of residual anger about the poll tax. And the residents of that leafy suburb – who were precisely the voters that the Tories were most worried about losing – had no sympathy at all with the riots, and relatively little with the non-payment campaign. There are important lessons here. For one thing, as you rightly imply, the non-payment campaign didn't amount to a mass movement; or, rather, it remained a mass movement that was entirely confined to communities and localities which were already Labour strongholds.

What do we learn from this? Well, the same old lessons that an unreformed Gramscian like me tends to draw from every such situation: you need a broad-based coalition and a language that the different elements of that coalition can more or less share; riots get you nowhere in this country, because the idea that they are a fundamentally illegitimate form of protest runs too deep in the British political psyche. To make things happen you need at least some degree of resonance between organised 'street level' resistance and a serious electoral challenge to the status quo. Probably the most important thing missing from our current situation is a clearly defined alternative agenda from Labour that will put real electoral pressure on the coalition; but we also need something more like the sustained participatory campaigning of the anti-poll tax movement, and less focus on spectacular but inevitably short-term interventions (demonstrations, occupations).

On the issue of how to avoid left ghettoisation in following the anti-capitalist logic of activists' convictions – one thing they need to do is to put together a coherent and realistic programme, and to pressure the Labour leadership to take a position on it. This in no way precludes other kinds of activity. It seems to me that time and again we can learn this same lesson from the history of oppositional politics in the UK: what works is a combination of imaginative, peaceful, constructive, grassroots activism with a clear electoral alternative to the status quo. You don't have to co-ordinate them fully. We don't need Ed Miliband to say he supports the students, but we do need him to propose to implement a coherent alternative which looks more or less like something they would want. But if you ignore the need to hold together a broad-based coalition, and you try to insist on the right to violent protest, then you just get nowhere.

We've already seen this with UK Uncut's refusal to distance themselves from the Black Bloc. Sorry to say so – but they blew it. They had built up a good level of public support for their campaign, including swathes of the public and individuals as unlikely as Polly Toynbee, which was truly impressive; but when it came down to it, they were more bothered about being loyal to their anarchist principles than about holding on to that support, and in the process they threw away a historic opportunity. And their defence of their position collapsed into an absurd defence of liberal individualism: 'it's just up to every individual to decide for themselves how to act'. No it bloody isn't! The whole point of collective action is that it involves a degree of shared responsibility. Of course I understand why they took that position. But this is the kind of choice you have to make when you're trying to change the world: do you stay in your comfortable anarchist ghetto or do you maintain the precarious, difficult dialogue with the people on the middle ground who are starting to listen to you?

Another issue we've touched on in thinking about the specific lessons that one cohort of political actors can learn from the experience of a previous cohort (I'm deliberately avoiding the loaded and frequently-misleading term 'generation' here) is the even more fundamental one: *what is the mechanism by which such lessons could be learned at all?* The findings of research on the topic of cross-cohort knowledge transmission amongst activist groups are pretty depressing: they tend to show that successive cohorts face almost identical situations, problems and issues, and they learn almost nothing from the experience of previous cohorts, because there is simply no institutionalised mechanism by which they could be shared.

It seems to me that this is a huge problem for the postmodern, networked politics which some student activists have been so enthusiastic about. In an age without mass political parties – when the job of parties is to reproduce professional political elites and to win elections through clever media strategies, rather than to organise democratic publics – then it is very unclear what kind of organisation could actually carry out some of the crucial historic functions of parties: enabling, containing and delimiting broad-based coalitions in a way which prevents their militant wings from inevitably spiralling off into irrelevance, and their centrist wings from lapsing into abject conservatism; constituting sites of public debate at which large-scale social analysis and long-term goals can come together with pragmatic and localised forms of policy-making and problem-solving; and constituting and preserving the institutional memory of a movement. It's this last function which I'm bemoaning the lack of today. We're already seeing interesting experiments in addressing the first two: Compass, in particular, is exciting for its attempt to carry out the first two of these functions. So I'll stick to thinking about the third.

Preserving and writing the movement's history can nourish a real sense of historical consciousness: a sense of the specificity, contingency, but also the continuity of one's particular historical situation. One worry is that we no longer have the equivalents of the radical historiography that was carried out in the postwar period up to 1970s, and that it isn't seen as important. What would enable us to historicise our own situation in this way, to produce and sustain the kind of knowledge that we need? It's really striking that this is the kind of thing that the Communist Party used to be really good at, and so the question remains: how do we do it in an age when there cannot be a Communist Party? Indeed, it's important to remember that even the Labour Party has fulfilled this kind of function within living memory. I will never forget being advised to read *The Ragged Trousered Philanthropists* by a 70-year-old member of my Labour Party branch when I was 18 years old. The question is: where could something like that happen today? I assume you will agree that if there is no place for such things to happen, there can ultimately be no successful political movement?

Perhaps the answer is that this is exactly the kind of thing that should form the content of new kinds of educational and research initiative outside of the increasingly neoliberalised formal education sector, that what we should be doing is trying to organise lecture series, research projects, seminars, podcasts, web-archives, precisely on the subject of radical history.

On the issue of the material interests represented by the tuition fees campaign, I would argue that the campaign ignored a rather uncomfortable socio-historical truth: namely that the new system of student funding only represents a dramatic reversal for those students who come from social groups wherein it has remained the normal expectation that parents would be able to fund their children to the completion of a university degree without incurring sizeable debts. Of course lots of poor students were brought onto the streets by the belief that the new system would actually mean that they had to find £27,000 up front to go to university, or would have to repay their loans at market rates on graduation (neither of which is remotely true), and by the abolition of the EMA (which is a real issue and had real effects, as I gladly concede). But that doesn't alter the fact that this was overwhelmingly a movement by and for the children of the professional classes.

For students from poorer backgrounds, the real difference between finishing university with a debt over £30,000 (as most of them do already) and one over £50,000 (as the new system implies) is largely abstract, and will be massively offset anyway by the fact that their loan repayments will now start only when they are earning over £21,000 a year instead of £15,000, and will be limited to a fixed proportion of their income. This is of course irrelevant to those students who confidently expect to earn more than £25,000 pa on graduation anyway: in other words, middle-class students at elite universities. For such students, fees until now have been sufficiently modest that parents could in many cases hope to be able to subsidise or cover both fees and living expenses such that their children wouldn't have to graduate with massive debts. The whole idea of starting your working life debt-free (or even with that nice little nest egg which grandma bequeathed to you still intact) has in fact been an exclusively middle-class privilege for a whole generation now (and working-class life under capitalism has involved routine indebtedness throughout its history, with the only exception being the post-war generation). And this was what the campaign was really about: the professional classes are furious that the historic privilege of entering the labour market unencumbered by debt is being withdrawn from them. You can't tell me that *this* wasn't something we heard endlessly during the campaign: 'these reforms mean that I will start working life with a massive debt around my neck' – as if this hadn't been the norm for students from poor backgrounds for decades already. Framing things in these terms revealed a constitutive blindness to the real class issues at stake; the campaign can be characterised as exclusionary in that it really had nothing to say to those groups who had *never* enjoyed the privilege of free, full-time, state-funded, debt-free higher education. The campaign should have been predicated on a much stronger critique of the existing funding arrangements – which have for years been marginalising and under-supporting working-class students – and on the implicit elitism of the entire HE funding system, which is predicated on the assumption that such inequalities are not only acceptable but desirable.

None of this is to say that the professional classes don't have the right to defend their own interests; but it is to suggest that the campaign was always far more of a sectional defence of a relatively narrow set of interests than it ever wanted to admit to itself, and that this self-delusion was fundamental to its inability to widen out its social and critical scope. I really think the movement can't develop or go forward until it gets to grip with this set of issues, instead of kidding itself that the rights which it is trying to defend were ever previously very widely enjoyed.

Guy: Underlying all of these issues is the perennial question of how the left organises when its traditional institutions are dead or in decline. The stakes couldn't be much higher. At the time of writing the entire Eurozone is in danger of financial collapse. Everywhere popular sovereignty and living standards are being sacrificed to the gods of the market, with our own government now blaming Europe for the disastrous impact of its own policy of retrenchment.

But there are also signs of hope. It seems more and more clear that we are entering an era of mass anti-capitalist protests. Occupations, strikes, popular assemblies, economic blockades and outbursts of civil unrest are fast becoming the familiar backdrop to the breakdown of Globalisation 2.0. It's all a bit bewildering. For years, neoliberalism promoted the commonsense view that any kind of collective action is futile. Now, all of a sudden, it feels like Pandora's Box has been opened.

The new movements springing up bear many of the characteristics you attribute to the student movement of 2010. Contentious politics are enacted with little reference to any established body of theory or practice. We see established institutional actors being sidelined. Broad swathes of the population are undergoing a rapid process of politicisation and practical learning through experimentation. This is a strength in so far as it encourages creativity and openness. But there is a danger of failing to learn past lessons and quickly becoming demoralised. So the question of institutional memory is a pertinent one.

We could talk here about out how networked, rhizomatic forms of organisation, encouraged by what Aaron Peters and myself have termed the 'open-sourcing' of political activism, are well suited to short energetic bursts, whilst bureaucratic, arborescent forms allow for long-term strategy development, learning and planning. The role of the internet in lowering the barriers to collective action and undermining institutional monopolies over dissent is familiar. But does it also have a role to play in transmitting knowledge of strategy and tactics to new political actors? I'd tentatively suggest it does. Take the worldwide 'Occupy' protests inspired by the Wall Street encampment and the Spanish *indignados*. The global mobilisation that took place on 15 October involved hundreds of thousands of people taking part in an estimated 951 actions in 82 countries.

Some on the left dispute the efficacy of these largely symbolic protests, but what can't be denied is that whereas previously it would have taken months, if not years, for news of the public encampments to spread and global co-ordination to take place, now it happens almost instantly, as protest tactics and repertoires that are judged successful spread virally like memes. The initial UK Uncut actions and student occupations had this quality, as do the nationwide walkouts and pickets by electricians who are seeing their pay cut by a third. A kind of collective learning is taking place. In *Rules for Radicals*, Saul Alinsky advises readers not to become impatient with the conservatism of new activists, since you can always rely on the reaction of the establishment to radicalise them. In an era of interconnected memetic activism this process is being fast-tracked, and the rules are changing. When police brutally cracked down on occupiers in Oakland, inflicting brain damage on an Iraq war veteran, this felt like a radicalising moment for the occupations movement globally. In response, thousands of activists shut down Oakland port – the fifth largest in America – with the co-operation of Longshoremen. It struck a more effective blow to US capital than any amount of smashing high-street banks. Millions around the globe watched, thanks to citizen reportage and the dissemination of the successful action on social media. Within the student movement, too, lessons are transmitted, as, for example, with Chile, where resistance to neoliberal reform of universities has exploded into a powerful mass movement, forcing President Pinera to point out that 'a demonstration is one thing, but trying to paralyse the country is something else entirely'.

Perhaps the meme of occupying ports will now catch on. Certainly there is an abundance of historical resources on economic blockades online, as well as instant analysis of what worked well and what didn't. The official public sphere, mediated by the corporate media, has been bypassed in favour of an unofficial cosmopolitan public sphere of networked anti-austerity struggles. Where this is heading no one can say. Chances are they will lose steam or get shut down by the authorities. That's what usually happens. But a seed has been planted. The occupations have provided a space to practice new co-operative forms of democratic citizenship, but also to discuss and demystify the reigning economic orthodoxy and imagine alternatives. The '99%' slogan may be woolly and unsophisticated as class analysis goes, but it crucially defines an antagonism, singling out the political and economic elites whose dominion has gone unchallenged for too long. Class power, long dormant, is being reconfigured.

Perhaps here I should probe your claim that targeted property damage will always be counter-productive under present conditions with a counter factual (leaving aside, for the time being, whether it counts as 'violence'). The Health and Social Care Bill, now in its final stages, will effectively privatise and dismantle the NHS, perhaps the single most popular institution in the country. The official opposition, organised by the trade unions, has had all the vigour and urgency of a sedated tortoise. Had there been a rambunctious street protest - perhaps even the smashing of a few windows – at the first stages of the parliamentary bill, as happened with Millbank, do you think a successful opposition movement to save the NHS would have been more or less likely? I'd suggest the former. Certainly it couldn't have done much worse than the 'candle-lit vigil' that was organised before the reforms had even passed. This isn't an endorsement of 'black bloc' tactics (I agree they probably alienated people on 26 March), more of a warning against uncritical genuflection before the semantics of 'peaceful' protest.

We are, I think, witnessing only the beginning of the popular reaction to the financial crisis of 2008. There were more than ten years between the Wall Street crash of 1929 and the new epoch of Keynesianism and the welfare state. The intervening period saw protest, social unrest, labour militancy and a world war. It's possible we're looking at a similar timescale before any watershed today, but it doesn't seem too implausible to suggest that information abundance and communications efficiency, alongside the speed of global markets, will quicken the pace of change.

I don't want to get too carried away here. The internet is no panacea. I doubt, for example, that it can replace the kind of formative, political education you received as a young man encouraged to read *The Ragged Trousered Philanthopists*. And the dissemination of activist 'best practice' globally is unlikely to substitute for the confidence that comes with a proud history of victories. It's also the case that the exhilarating peaks of collective agency we're seeing – 'moments of excess' in the words of the Freedom Association – aren't enough without the long-term infrastructure that empowers people in their everyday lives. I agree with you that if mainstream political parties ever did play a useful role in providing a shared history and culture, they no longer do so. The technocratic, centralised and hollowed out entities they have become are well described in political science as 'cartel parties' - not an outgrowth of civil society but an appendage of the state and corporations. It is the Trotskyist parties, of course, who always claimed to embody the 'historical memory' of the working class. Though they can play a useful role in educating radical youth, and encouraging union militancy, their out-dated Leninist dogma and hierarchical methods remain unpopular. It is noticeable how, unlike in 1968, there has not been a growth in the numbers of far left organisations.

Trade unions still provide a vital space where knowledge and skills are transmitted. Though weakened, the big unions, under pressure from the rank and file, still have the capacity to co-ordinate mass strike action involving millions of workers. Meanwhile, more radical, syndicalist unions have had some success in organising low-paid cleaners at the University of London and Guildhall. The boldness and adaptability of these groups could make them a model for today's struggles: Paul Mason's history of labour organising, *Live Working or Die Fighting*, demonstrates that the unions made their biggest gains before the era of centralised bureaucracies and full-timers. This is especially important when you consider that all but the most ineffective forms of union activity may well be prohibited by the Coalition government. We recently saw the farce of a minister suggesting that public sector unions engage in a symbolic 'fifteen minute strike' over pensions. I would put this down to pure vindictiveness, but, given the widespread ignorance of the labour movement's role and history, who knows?

If anti-union laws are passed, it will be consistent with a wider pattern of criminalising any dissent outside of institutionally prescribed channels. The new Metropolitan Police commissioner's strategy of Total Policing was put into effect at the student demonstration on 9 November 2011, when 4000 police, mounted units, dogs and undercover snatch squads were all deployed. Rubber bullets and water cannon, we were publicly warned, were on standby. All side streets were blocked and anyone who diverged from the official route was liable to arrest under draconian anti-protest laws. A mobile kettle herded us along the route through the City to Moorgate. Clearly the British state, too, has learned something from the last year of street protests. That's one place where institutional memory isn't an issue!

This means a new strategic situation. The National Campaign Against Fees and Cuts – a voluntary organisation – succeeded in putting 10,000 students on the streets on 9 November (a week-day), without the help of the NUS. Ideally, it will raise enough resources to become a nationally representative student organisation and keep its radicalism. But this move to a more conventional institutional politics amongst parts of the movement doesn't mean abandoning more confrontational tactics of collective action. Nor does it negate a more expressive politics that seeks to transform the norms, meanings and structures of civil society, the Gramsican 'common sense'.

An important part of this will involve exploring and challenging the role of debt in our society, and the way it structures and dominates our lives, disciplining us individually and collectively into the market. Insane plans are in the works to create a new securitised market out of student debt. It could well become the next subprime crisis. In the US, some estimates put student debt at $1 trillion. With loans being made at commercial rates and the state taking on the liabilities, it's a huge form of corporate welfare. In *Debt: The first 5000 years*, anthropologist David Graeber argues that whenever you have a huge expansion of virtual credit, you either have to have a safety valve of forgiveness or you have an intense outbreak of social violence that tears society apart. Under the Ancient Jewish Law of Jubilee all debts were automatically cancelled every seven years 'in the Sabbath year', and all those in debt bondage freed. It's something to consider. With the coming university intake in England paying the higher rates of fees, perhaps we will see the rise of non-payment unions (if a way can be found round the government's extraction of payments through the PAYE system), and a campaign for debt forgiveness to involve all current and former students.

I agree that last year's protests weren't anywhere near representative enough given the issues at stake. Part of this, as you say, was a result of class blindness and the failure to articulate demands that resonate with less well off students who already face a mountain of debt, or to acknowledge the existing bias and inequalities in higher education. As I'm sure you know, at London Metropolitan University, which has the largest working-class intake of any university, management are colluding with government to enforce cuts of 70 per cent, basically transforming it into a business school. It signifies what's happening to non-elite universities nationally: the removal of courses that aren't profitable for private providers, and an effective prohibition on working-class students studying the humanities. Many people in the broader student movement supported the occupation at London Met, but it's true this side of the campaign has had little attention compared to the media-friendly narrative of middle-class students unhappy about fees.

There is, I think, a wider difficulty here that faces any anti-austerity campaign: the need to defend collective provision against neoliberal reform, whilst acknowledging that existing services are imperfect and often profoundly unjust. I doubt there's an easy answer to this, but I think part of it will involve the creation of autonomous social and political spaces to reimagine the role of education along more democratic, egalitarian lines. There also needs be an intellectual effort to address the full scope of what is wrong with the current system along the lines of Michael Bailey and Des Freedman's *Assault on the Universities: A Manifesto for Resistance* and the *Alternative White Paper* by the Campaign for the Public University.

We know what we're fighting against. It's distilled in A.C. Grayling's New College of the Humanities that opens in Bloomsbury in 2012 - a grotesque boutique college for the global ultra rich, where share-holding celebrity dons fly in for the occasional lecture whilst academic proles do the drudge work. It's a sign of things to come unless we build an effective, broad-based campaign to fight privatisation.

Guy Aitchison is a writer and political activist currently studying for a PhD in Political Theory at UCL. His research focuses on how the content and scope of rights is collectively decided, with a special emphasis on the role of social movements. He has been active in the student movement and wider anti-cuts movement and is a regular contributor to openDemocracy's UK section, OurKingdom.

Jeremy Gilbert teaches Cultural Studies at the University of East London and has written widely on politics, music and cultural theory. His most recent book is *Anticapitalism and Culture* (Berg, 2008).

Organising with others, not for them

George Gabriel

We have learned to be suspicious. Our experience of the political parties who claim to represent the have-nots is that those who pledged, promised and pronounced have been cowed, co-opted and corrupted. We will not forget marching against Iraq, being sold out on tuition fees, or mortgaging our futures to pay for the greed and excess of the greedy and excessive. We are less likely to join a political party than our parents and less likely to vote for one than any previous electorate in British history.

We are suspicious of the two traditional pillars of British civil society: faith and labour. Unforgiving of their political compromises, and rubbed raw by their glacial bureaucratic processes, we are less likely to join a trade union than any other generation in the last hundred years. At the same time fewer of our generation than any before sit on a pew each Sunday, joining a church which seems to have spent the life of our generation gazing at an ugly navel – women priests and gay bishops, are they really the priority when children live in poverty and violence stalks our streets? What path does the radical chart in a public life so diminished?

While suspicious of our allies we're certain of the enemy. We have seen the might of financial capital and big business bring the world economy to its knees, throw 20 per cent of our generation into unemployment, and devastate the hopes and aspirations we harboured for decent and dignified lives. To us this is not abstract; it's a friend who doesn't get up until two in the afternoon unless forced to by the benefits office. It's spending months sleeping on sofas because we can't afford to pay rents in the few cities where we might be fortunate enough to find work. It's working as 'interns' – interned in unpaid work.

The truth is that our generation hates elites, whatever their colour. Today's radical understands that a struggle between left and right elites is not our own. We want to smash down the edifice upon which both stand, not join their ranks. So how do we organise? How do we as radicals achieve change while suspicious of institutions and leaders who claim to act on our behalf?

One response has been exile from public life. We choose exile over equivocation, isolationism over indignity and construction over conflict. We choose to try and create perfectly sustainable, vegan, egalitarian, multicultural, communes. We don't give up our values, choosing to realise them if not in public life then at least in our own. We choose to 'be changed' because frankly we lack the means to 'be the change'.

The truth is that we young radicals are not the change we've been waiting for. For our suspicion of institutions and leadership, we risk throwing baby, mother, public life and society out with the bath water. The challenge of achieving change under the threat of compromise, co-option and corruption is overcome not by giving up on real change, but by achieving it *with* people – not *for* them. That is the challenge facing today's radical, who wants not to concentrate power in their own hands, or the hands of another, but rather see it shared, democratised. It's said that 'If you want to do something different you have to be different'. For our generation the opposite holds: 'If you want to be different you have to do something differently!'.

Social media – the radical and rapid growth of network – has given us new tools to organise. We are more networked than ever before, increasing our ability to rapidly respond to crisis. We are horizontally linked, without mediation, interpretation or aggregation. We raise standards in the air and see who will get behind them – an effective tool for re-action – expressing outrage or spreading example. But building lasting institutions that continue the fight beyond the crisis through network has so far proved difficult: from Arab Spring to Anti-cuts. What we have is ultimately a platform in which anyone can lead, but not for long. And how will that last and evolve? Does an escalation of networks, presuming even our generation's indefatigable interest in connection doesn't tire, sufficiently transform public life? Sufficiently increase our ability to act? Sufficiently democratise power in British society?

Community organising argues ardently and urgently for the additional need for an opposite style of organisation: we bring people together and then decide together what standard we want to raise. We fiercely believe true democratic self governance is our best hope to end the injustices we live with, the one path between the world as it is and the world as it should be. The radical is suspicious of elites – our task is therefore not to lead public life, but to facilitate the participation of others: agitating; equipping; educating; relating to the vast majority of people who have been pushed out of the polity, commodified by markets, and infantilised and betrayed by the state and those who control it.

Community organising's explicit purpose is the building of power alliances of institutions, bringing diverse groups together across divides to formulate a common agenda which together they're powerful enough to pursue for the common good. If popular religion and trade unionism saw faith-based organising and work-based organising for justice, place-based organising is fundamentally the work of community organisers. Churches, trade unions, mosques, charities, housing associations, synagogues and schools may not share much, but they do share a place. From this basis of shared self interest, community organisers facilitate and agitate towards common action. From common action on shared self interest we progress to common action for the common good. To change the world we better live in it, we must go to people where they are and not where we would like them to be. This is even the case with the very same institutions we are suspicious of.

The pre-eminent organisation in Britain for community organising is London Citizens, an alliance of 200 such institutions, and more latterly Citizens UK, as community organising has begun to expand beyond the capital.

The process is at times painfully slow. It may take years to develop sufficiently strong relationships with leaders of the diverse groups that share a city to get them in a room together. An organiser then might ask what makes them angry – angry people will act. 'Poverty' – well 'poverty' is too big, you aren't strong enough to take on poverty, let's break it down.

The leaders will leave, go back to their institutions and work out the nature of poverty in their area – asking their people how poverty affects them, what it means and what they'd want to see done about it. Ten years ago a similar group reconvened and found that for the communities they represented in East London, poverty wasn't so much a story of unemployment, as low pay. The cost of living was such that people worked in up to three jobs to keep up: up at 4am, catch the bus which takes double the time because you can't afford the tube, work till midday, two hours off, which is never enough time to make it home and back so you wait, back on till ten, catch the bus which takes double the time because you can't afford the tube, asleep at midnight, up at 4am ...

Community organisers look for simple, common-sense solutions to these problems that anyone can understand, and that come close to meeting the interests of all. That day the Living Wage campaign in the UK was born – the simple idea that those working full time deserve to live with dignity, and so wages should at least reflect the minimum required to get by. But organisers don't just raise a standard and see who will get behind it; they ask where the people in our institutions are, and who it is who's paying these shamefully low wages. Canary Wharf rapidly became the target – as bankers' bonuses were taking off, their cleaners and security guards were being left behind, but London Citizens wasn't powerful enough to take them all on: HSBC became the target. But buildings don't change their minds: organisers know you need a person. Community organising doesn't deal with underlings. Companies and governments employ legions to keep people away from the decision-makers, through stakeholder meetings, consultations, forums, CSR and customer service; their purpose is to tire people out before they get to power's door – London Citizens picked Sir John Bond, then Chair of HSBC as its target.

The organisers and the leaders of the institutions they were working with wrote to Sir John asking for a meeting – no reply. Phoned his office and were brushed off. They took action. The institutions saved up copper coins for months and on the busiest hour of the busiest day of the year they went to the flagship HSBC branch to change them. Priests, trade unionists and teachers opened accounts only to close them. Out comes the manager breathing fire. 'Calm down' the leaders say, 'we're reasonable people and just want you to pick up the phone, ring head office, and urge them to meet with us to discuss pay and conditions'. To his credit he picked up the phone … and called the police. No cause for arrest but they're thrown out with no meeting.

What's next? What action might get the reaction you want – a meeting with Sir John Bond? Organisers understand that you don't act for action's sake, you take action to get a reaction, and we wanted to get in the room where the decision would be made. Leaders and organisers within London Citizens bought shares in HSBC and went to the AGM, where they stood opposite Sir John Bond as he was about to justify his remuneration package for the year and said, 'Shame on you Sir John, for the poverty wages you pay people like Abdul', at which point Abdul Durant – a cleaner who worshipped at East London Mosque – stood up and said:

> Sir John, it's an honour to work for a man like you. You may not know this but I clean your office, and though we work in the same building we live in different worlds. You're going to go home and consider what to do with your two million pound

bonus; I'm going home to my wife where we'll discuss how on
earth we're going to afford a new school uniform for our
daughter.

Under all this pressure Sir John, when asked, agrees to meet, and at
that meeting the first toehold for the Living Wage in Canary Wharf
was won.

The Living Wage campaign has now won £70 million in extra
wages for working people in London. That is huge and important,
but it is not the point – the point is the development of a powerful
alliance of institutions permanently able to act on the issues that
affect its members; the point is the entering into public life of Abdul
Durant. Similar stories can be told of fights to save street lighting,
replace broken security doors on run-down estates, tackle knife
crime, run damp out of social housing. All this work matters, but
the point is the development of a powerful alliance of leaders,
united across traditional divides by strong bonds of solidarity and
self interest, bonds forged in common action.

A famous bank robber was once asked why he robbed banks,
'Because that's where the money is', he replied. Community
organisers build power among the have-nots because that's where it
isn't. We must be prepared to meet them where they are and not just
where we'd like them to be. This pragmatic radicalism was first
articulated by Saul Alinsky, a Jewish community organiser who
began his work in Chicago seventy years ago and wrote the seminal
text *Rules for Radicals*; this book remains as powerful today as ever,
and is one of the only coherent visions for the revitalisation of public
life in democratic societies.

And of radicals? Few are on our side, we are our own partisans.
Only by organising with others, and not for them, meeting people
where they are, and not where we'd like them to be, can we be the
change we want to see in the world – the creation of a living,
breathing British democracy.

George Gabriel has worked for three years as a community organiser with Citizens UK to build power and relationships in civil society – work he began after spending a year immersed in Venezuelan social movements, from where he returned only to witness, with anger, the election of the BNP to the European parliament. A passionate democrat, George has been active across the democratic reform sector, co-founding Take Back Parliament, and leading in other campaigns to change the structures of British democracy while working to organise its substance.

The children of the children of the revolution

Tim Gee

Young people are on the front line of struggles for social justice across the globe. The Arab Spring of 2011 inspired a new wave of resistance, including the *indignados* in Spain, street camps in Israel, then city centre camps across the world as part of the global Occupy movement. But a downside to the way that events in North Africa have been reported is a myth that if people simply occupy the streets for long enough, change will eventually follow. There is of course a correlation, and street protest is important. But change does not automatically follow. For 'people power' to be effective it needs to directly challenge the interests of the powerful.

The tactics of the Arab Spring did not come from nowhere. At least in part they can be traced back to the youth led movement against Slobodan Milosevic in Serbia in 2000.[1] These in turn were influenced by the work of the scholar Gene Sharp, who has dedicated his life to examining the dynamics of social change. In his most influential work *From Dictatorship to Democracy*, he calls upon the reader to identify the 'Achilles' heel' of the regime it is campaigning against, and to find ways to undermine elites' sources of power. If we are to learn from the source rather than the myth, we must take note.

Resistance to the power of elites requires the deployment of Counterpower, of which there are three broad categories. The first, 'Idea Counterpower', can be exercised by challenging accepted truths, refusing to obey and finding new channels of communication. The second, 'Economic Counterpower', can be exercised through strikes, boycotts and ethical consumption. The third, 'Physical Counterpower' can on occasion manifest itself through literal fighting, although the route of non-violent direct action is far more preferable. Movements that use two or three kinds of Counterpower are more likely to succeed than those that use only one. But more importantly, the greatest changes come when movements find ways to undermine the physical, economic and ideological power of elites.

Another legend growing up around the uprising in Egypt is that it took place because of the internet. In an interview with *New Internationalist*, the revolutionary Gigi Ibrahim dismissed such claims: 'Yes, we used the internet to communicate and spread information, but if the struggle wasn't there, if the people didn't take to the streets, if the factories didn't shut down, if workers didn't go on strike, none of this would have happened'.[2] Ibrahim encapsulates the major elements of Counterpower, including the Economic Counterpower of strike action and the Physical Counterpower of action on the streets. But the importance of communicating alternative ideas cannot be underestimated either. As Egyptian blogger Hossam El-Hamalawy puts it: 'In dictatorship, independent journalism by default becomes a form of activism. The spread of information is essentially an act of agitation.'[3]

Young people in Britain may not be taking on a dictatorship, at least not as popularly defined. But neither do we live in a democracy where young people have control over our lives. There is a growing gap between *haves* and *have-nots* which correlates with age, reflected in the figures. Those of us born after 1979 are less likely to own a house, less likely to get a car, and less likely to get a job, than the previous generation when they were our age. In 1990, 50 per cent of people under thirty-five owned houses. Now it is just 29 per cent. Since the economic crisis, youth unemployment has rocketed. Amongst those aged eighteen to twenty-five it is now 1 in 5.[4]

Fellow contributor Shiv Malik calls those of us born after Thatcher's Conservatives came to power in 1979 the 'Jilted Generation'. Yet we have now seen three political parties in government. Every one of them has been wedded to the same ideology of neoliberalism which has let us down so badly, and, if allowed to continue, will let the next generation down even more. But there are ways that we can resist.

Using Counterpower

In building Idea Counterpower we are on the front foot. UK Uncut has shown how Twitter and Facebook can be used not only to inform but to empower, and how carefully designed creative confrontations can mould the mainstream media narrative. We are also steadily democratising the media by *becoming* the media. Many of the top blogs, as defined by the Wikio and Total Politics rankings, are written by young people, some of whom are contributing to this volume. Indeed, some of them – such as Political Scrapbook and Liberal Conspiracy – even contributed to the downfall of the News of the World by driving the campaign for companies to pull their advertising: an instructive example of Idea Counterpower merging with Economic Counterpower to undermine the interests of elites.

This aside, most young people do not have a great deal of experience of the traditional forms of Economic Counterpower. Strikes are of course impossible without employment. Even amongst those with jobs, trade union membership is painfully low amongst the young. Reversing this – as well as fighting for greater democracy within trade unions – must be a priority. Prospects for a tuition fee non-payment campaign modelled on the successful anti-poll tax movement are frustrated by the government's policy of extracting tuition fees through pay packets.

What we are well placed to organize is Physical Counterpower. For example, this could be manifested in the struggle for free education, if groups of people unable to afford education arrived at universities and – with the support of existing students – demanded to be taught. Again, the Physical, Economic, and Idea Counterpower of sustained action on these lines could bring far more pressure to bear than the speeches and demonstrations that currently characterise the tactics of many student unions.

The 2010 occupation of Millbank Tower – home to the offices of the Conservative Party – is an example of Physical and Idea Counterpower successfully merging. Although polls after the event suggested that the public generally disapproved, the Conservatives fell to second place in the opinion polls the following day and remained there for the succeeding months.[5] But it is not only the Tories that have let down the young: Labour and the Liberal Democrats have too. Surely the next step would be to occupy the offices of all neoliberal political parties in order to undermine their power.

But what of mainstream politics and the increasingly undemocratic parties and pressure groups overseen by our elders? It is little surprise that in such a context, many young people are attracted to non-hierarchical social movements. In the face of the perceived slowness and incrementalism of bureaucratic institutions, many young people prefer – in the words of one recent documentary – to 'Just Do It'. The National Campaign Against Fees and Cuts, Climate Camp and UK Uncut are just three of the groups that have emerged in such circumstances. Yet despite the vibrancy and effectiveness of such light-footed grassroots organisations, few manage to endure the passing of time compared to more established institutions.

Yet this is not a new tension. In the 1940s, Nelson Mandela viewed the ANC of the time as 'the preserve of a tired, unmilitant, privileged African elite'.[6] In response, the Congress Youth League was formed. Their proposed tactics against the government included boycotts, strikes and civil disobedience. The Youth League informed their elders that they would only back candidates for positions within the ANC who supported a more militant approach. Although they were condemned they eventually began to change the organisation, and the nature of the struggle.

Those of us who are involved in the youth wings of political parties and pressure groups have something to learn, beginning by asking who our allegiance is to – our generation or the older leadership. If it is to our generation we must take every opportunity to oppose, stand against, out, expose and ultimately remove those careerists who place neoliberal economics above the principles of intergenerational justice.

Yet to only engage through institutions amounts to a reduction in our power. On this point the seminal organisers Bill Moyer and Saul Alinsky offer sage advice. Moyer argues that, in the early stage of campaigns, participants should use mainly constitutional means – not because they will make a difference, but to show how the *haves* are preventing the democratic system from operating democratically. Alinsky advises that fundamental change only takes place when the people feel 'so futureless in the prevailing system that they are willing to let go of the past and chance the future'.[7] To some extent our power also relies on us chancing the future.

Young people

The struggle can be hard, but young people are well placed to rise to the challenge for a number of reasons, of which three are particularly prominent. Firstly, young people have time. Social change can take a long time and involve losing a lot of campaigns. As the South African revolutionary Joe Slovo put it: 'Until the moment of successful revolutionary take-over, each individual act of resistance usually fails … the rare moment in history which makes possible the final victorious revolutionary assault is a compound of a people and a movement with an accumulated heritage of resistance, which, through all the immediate "failures", perpetuates and reinforces the tradition of struggle'.[8]

Secondly, young people have communities in which resistance can be built. Young people are more likely to be in full-time education than other people, and be more accustomed to using social network sites, which allow for a greater flow of people to be involved in movement activities.

Perhaps most importantly, young people have very little to lose. The youth riots of 2011 showed that large numbers of young people feel so disenfranchised by the system, and so desensitised by police violence and oppression, that they are no longer scared of challenging it. This spirit was also present in the 2010 occupation of Conservative Party headquarters, which, in the words of one participant, represented 'the expression of a generation at the end of its tether'.[9]

Yet the fact that other groups are also disadvantaged by the current regime – including the working class elderly – means that our antagonism cannot be towards the previous generation *per se*, but to the ideas and decisions of unaccountable elites, whose power has grown in recent decades. The growth of corporate power has increased CEOs' stranglehold over the economy. The rise of managerialism within political parties has consolidated power with the few and closed down democratic channels once central to our system. Even within many civil society organisations there exists a dictatorship of the old and privileged which can serve to stifle the energy and perspectives of more youthful members. What we need is not inter-generational conflict but cross-generational solidarity in resisting the concentration of power.

Many of our parents opposed this shift to the right. They were part of the anti-poll tax movement, the miners' strike, the anti-apartheid league, the women's movement, the anti-nuclear movement and, perhaps most iconically, the multi-issue uprisings of 1968. There is much to learn from these admirable struggles. But it would be also be naïve to be uncritical towards them. We are the children of the children of the revolution. We are keen to learn from our predecessors' successes. But we are also determined not to repeat their mistakes.

Of course there is an important difference. Unlike struggles based primarily on race, gender, disability or class, the young of today will not always be young. We will, however, always be post-1979ers – the people who, in our youth at least, only knew neoliberalism. It must be our mission to ensure that our children have a choice. And we will only know that we have been successful when our children rise up to challenge us where we have not gone far enough.

Tim Gee is the author of *Counterpower: Making Change Happen* (2011). He delivers training sessions for political activists. Tim studied Politics at Edinburgh University, where he was also active in the student movement.

Notes

1. Serbian activist Srdga Popovic advised the Egyptian April 6 Youth Movement.
2. Phil England, 'Fear no more', newint.org/features/web-exclusive/2011/04/20/egypt-revolution-gigi/.
3. Hossam El-Hamalawy's blog is at: http://www.arabawy.org/blog/.
4. See Shiv Malik and Ed Howker, *Jilted Generation*, Icon Books, 2010.
5. Whether this was coincidental or due to the main demonstration is a matter that would require further research. What is does indicate, though, is that it did not undermine the cause, and may even have boosted it as it precipitated a new wave of protest in the weeks that followed.
6. Nelson Mandela, *Long Walk to Freedom*, Abacus, 1995.
7. Saul Alinksy, *Rules for Radicals*, Vintage, 1989.
8. Joe Slovo et al, *The New Politics of Revolution in Southern Africa*, Pelican, 1976.
9. Sam Coates, co-chair of Young Greens, cited in: brightgreenscotland.org/index.php/2010/11/this-is-the-expression-of-a-generation-at-the-end-of-its-tetheryoung-greens/.

A *botellon sin alcohol*: the *indignados* and the re-invention of public sociability

Paolo Gerbaudo

When I first arrived at the *indignados* protest camp at Puerta del Sol in Madrid it was a Saturday night, six days after the first demonstration called by the group *Democracia Real Ya*, on 15 May 2011. The streets around the geographic centre of the capital (the *kilometro zero* of the nation) were filled to capacity by a lively and noisy crowd. Such a scene is in fact anything but exceptional in this area, which is the heartland of Madrid's tapas bars and the local *movida* (nightlife); locals and tourists flock to its *tavernas* to drink beer and wine, and eat small plates of *chorizo, jamon, pulpo a la gallega* and other local delights.

What was impressive for me on that night was not the presence of a crowd but its nature and its spirit. Groups of people were holding banners and posters, with hand-written messages attacking bankers, big national corporations like Endesa and Banco Santander, and the political class from left to right: no-one was excluded. Instead of the drunken chants one often hears in a place like this at this time of the week I heard slogans like *no me representan* (they don't represent me) and *lo llaman democracia y no lo es* (they called it democracy but it is not). But yet more surprising for me – whose only previous experience in Puerta del Sol was a binge-drinking night during a high school trip gone out of control – was the simple fact that people around me were not drinking!

Around us illegal street vendors seemed to be having quite a hard time finding customers for their chilled beer cans of the worst quality. When we finally managed to enter the square proper I was amazed to see a sober crowd of thousands of people streaming under the blue and green tents that had been erected between the two main fountains of Puerta del Sol. Small groups of people sat on the pavement of the square in animated discussion. But at the centre of those circles, where one would normally have expected to see a bottle of wine, beer or calimocho – that most unlikely wine-coca-cola cocktail – there was none.

Stewards methodically but gently reprimanded anybody who was not complying with the rule, while from time to time a person on the megaphone would reiterate the injunction: 'this is a protest, this is not a party, please do not drink in the square, please do not smoke joints'. A hand-written message stuck to one of the lamp-posts of the square made the prohibition official: *esto no es un botellon*. But save for the absence of alcohol, the situation in the square precisely mirrored the sociability of the *botellon* – a gathering of young people in a public space drinking cheap alcohol bought from a nearby supermarket – a practice which has recently been made illegal in several Spanish cities including Barcelona and Madrid.

The (protest) party is over

To understand the nature and power of the *indignados* anti-austerity protests which have taken place in Spain since 15 May 2011 (#15M), it is worth paying attention to this paradoxical nature of the gatherings it has created – a *botellon sin alcohol*, a *botellon* without alcohol. Such an apparently trivial detail is instructive about the novelty of this movement, and about its differences from previous cycles of protest, particularly from the anti-globalisation movement. Although we see in the *indignados* a resort to direct action and direct democracy that immediately recalls the practices of protests seen at counter-summits against the G8, the World Trade Organisation and the World Bank, there is a fundamental difference in their protest ethic: an ethic of pleasure sometimes bordering on self-indulgence has given way to one of duty and self-discipline.

The anti-globalisation protests will forever be associated with the practice of protest-parties, such as those inaugurated by the Reclaim the Streets movement in the UK in the mid-1990s. At the height of neoliberalism's dominance, and at the climax of the housing bubble – when the majority of citizens seemed to be satisfied with the status quo – it seemed to make sense to use the repertoire of festivals and raves as a form of protest against a system which combined consumerism with an underlying health-obsessed paternalism (no sugar, no caffeine, no cigarettes, no drugs). As a riposte to the exclusive parties of the brokers of the City and Wall Street, the movement arranged inclusive counter-cultural carnivals, displaying the creativity and indulgence that the system was constantly trying to capture – either to turn it into a commodity or to ruthlessly repress it.

Today, in the face of the widespread social distress caused by the global economic crisis, resorting to parties and festivity would be unlikely to resonate with the everyday experience of those taking to the streets. 'They want people to take this seriously, and avoid the media representing us as usual, as a bunch of *punkis*', explained Teresa, one of our Spanish friends. Those who have been involved in demonstrations in recent years know only too well how mainstream news media carefully dismiss any protest event as the action of hippies out of touch with the majority of the people. But in the days after the *indignados* movement erupted, media coverage in Spain was consistently positive; the more right-wing media had to put great effort into singling out the few drunkards, punks or homeless people in the crowd in order to convey the usual narrative of loony protesters.

The self-imposed prohibitions of the *indignados* did not simply have to do with attempting to avoid bad press – something that is often decisive in undermining the credibility of progressive social movements, as Todd Gitlin has shown in the *Whole World is*

Watching. The apparent moralism of the camp also stemmed from a widespread impression that heavy consumption of alcohol and drugs had contributed to slowing down young Spaniards' reaction to the economic crisis. '*Estabamos apalancados*' (we were stuck), asserted Lucia, a 25-year-old student. 'People were just trying to forget their problems, getting drunk every night'. Other protesters described their generation to me as being 'zombified', for a long time unable to react to its difficult situation because it was too spoiled and pampered, looking for private consolation from its existential troubles in the *movida*.

The self discipline of the *indignados* may create discomfort among some activists on the left: 'Isn't this all rather moralistic and paternalist?'. There is room for debate on the disciplinary implications of this practice, and its dangers, but it is important to note that, despite the prohibition of alcohol and drugs, the protest camp at Puerta del Sol was dominated by an atmosphere of enthusiasm and cordiality. Moreover, it is undeniable that setting a series of rules of conduct helped to ensure that the space of protest was hospitable towards people whom it would be rare to have encountered in anti-capitalist protests before the economic crisis. Waking up on Sunday morning after a sober Saturday night spent in the camp – with not even the slightest sign of a hangover – I was impressed to see pensioners, middle-aged women and families touring the protest camp and chatting with protesters. Local shop-keepers and inhabitants were bringing bags full of food, water, and other goodies that were all very much needed in the camp. Others were coming to express their solidarity, and to share their anger against the political and economic system.

'I am all in favour of what they are doing', stated Rosa, a 65-year-old retired teacher. 'I would do the same they are doing, because the bankers and politicians are thieves.' At the popular kitchen tent I met another pensioner, Esteban, who was intently distributing dishes to the crowd under the burning May sun. 'It is not just young people who have a problem,' he explained to me. 'If

you look at how much I get every month with my pension you will
see how dire is the condition of us older people'. In turn many
young people I interviewed underlined that it was not just a revolt of
youth (though youth constituted the great majority in the protest);
they wanted to build solidarity with older generations. 'We' re all in
the same shit', as many prosaically put it.

Soberness vs austerity

To understand the spirit of the *indignados* movement and the type of
public space it has constructed, it is worth referring to what, in my
opinion, is the slogan that best represents its novelty and its
difference from previous waves of protests. This is not the oft-
repeated *vamos lentos, porque vamos lejos* (we go slow because we go
far) – which can sound rather like a justification for the sluggishness
of direct consensus-based democracy. Rather, it is the alternative *no
somos anti-sistema, es el sistema que es contra nosotros*: to be translated
as 'We are not against the system, it is the system that is against us'.
This slogan – in common with that of Occupy Wall Street's 'we are
the 99%' – reflects the majoritarian spirit of this movement, its
ambition to represent the 'people', regardless of their political and
cultural affiliations.

The corollary of this brilliant reversal of the negative labelling
used by mainstream news media is the creation of a public space in
which the self-imposition of a number of prohibitions goes hand in
hand with an attempt at constructing new forms of popular
sociability, capable of involving the 'common people' or 'family
people' who for the most part were noticeably absent in the anti-
globalisation protests. These are people, who, regardless of their
level of militancy, have been made to pay for the consequences of
the current financial crisis, but do not necessarily share the
alternative life-styles of many young protesters. Thus the
prohibition of alcohol and drugs in the square can be read as part of
a new protest ethic which studiously avoids making an alternative

lifestyle a form of exclusion towards others: an attitude which has proved self-ghettoising on many occasions.

It is in this sense that the public space created by the *indignados* echoes the protest camp of Tahrir Square, from which it has drawn much inspiration. Many Egyptian activists I have been interviewing in recent months as part of a fieldwork study about new media and new spaces of protest in the Euro-Mediterranean area have asserted that Tahrir Square was a 'moral space', a space in which people behaved according to self-imposed rules. Thus, for example, in a society in which women undergo sexual harassment on a daily basis, it was remarkable how in the square itself women were pro-actively protected from male friction, and 'boys were surprisingly well behaved', as Sally, a 27-year old activist told me, when recounting her experience in the protests. Similarly the camp of the *indignados* in Puerta del Sol testified to an effort to create a moral space, which studiously avoided the indulgence associated with the wave of anti-globalisation protests and the format of protest-parties.

While the anti-globalisation movement re-appropriated the excess of neoliberalism to produce forms of public space centring on festivity, self-expression and entertainment, the *indignados* testify to a reversal of this trend. Austerity is turned into a self-imposed soberness, which is used to convey the 'seriousness' of the movement, the sharing of the participants in the sufferings of the people at large, and an awareness of a moment of collective crisis. At the same time, the movement is characterised by its own forms of festivity and pleasure-driven activity, but in a way which avoids creating symbolic boundaries that exclude 'ordinary' people. This effort entails recuperating and rethinking existing forms of alternative public sociability. In the case of the *indignados*, the format which has been re-appropriated has been the *botellon* – which, deprived of its essential ingredient, abundant and cheap alcohol, has been turned into a format of gathering open to people beyond the young activists' counter-cultural milieu: including the old, not to speak of teetotallers.

Paolo Gerbaudo is a media and cultural researcher interested in social movements and new media. His forthcoming book, *Tweeting from the Barricades* (Pluto, 2012), discusses the new forms of mobilisation emerging across a number of social movements, from the anti-globalisation movement to the Arab Spring, the *indignados* and Occupy.

UK Uncut: a case study in activism

Chris Coltrane

In the space of just half a year, UK Uncut grew from a forty person protest into one of the most recognised and popular anti-cuts groups in the country. Due to their direct action and media engagement, tax justice is now at the forefront of the austerity debate.

Unions, NGOs and campaign groups across the country are keen to understand the tactics UK Uncut used to succeed. Indeed, the lessons deserve to be shared with all campaigners, new and old. Firsthand experience of both attending and organising UK Uncut actions has given me an understanding of the essential tactics and strategies adopted by UK Uncut, and which other campaigners might do well to emulate.

1) Fun, original, exciting protests

Perhaps the most important starting point is the originality of the protests themselves. To summarise a typical demonstration: a group of activists enter a shop owned by a corporation accused of avoiding UK tax. Sometimes they simply sit down, blocking the doors, other times it involves theatre, such as transforming the store into a library, or a school sports day, and, on occasion, even the act of announcing an action is enough to close the store in advance – such is the power of a UK Uncut protest. The message is clear: if you avoid tax, we won't let you trade.

At the first demo against Vodafone on 27 October 2010, I live tweeted the protest from inside the shop. To my surprise, and sheer delight, thousands of people shared my tweets and photos. The reason it gained such a buzz was because, for many people, this was the most exciting protest they'd seen in years. It was new, and strikingly innovative. There was an energy and excitement which was almost unparalleled.

Occupations are a common tactic in the history of resistance, and direct action is employed by many other modern groups, such as Climate Camp, and NHS Direct Action. However, few can recall a time of direct action on a nationwide scale. The act of closing a shop was a bold, exciting and fresh approach, capturing people's attention and imagination.

But crucially, it wasn't just that the protests were original. Fun was woven deep into their fabric. We turned banks into libraries with comic, oversized books; Oxford hosted a Formula 1 race around all the tax avoiders in the town, with cars made out of cardboard boxes; Santa was filmed being arrested in Brighton; Topshop was transformed into a school sports day; and Boots into a hospital, complete with bleeding zombie-patients and prop medical equipment. It isn't hard to see why this would appeal to more participants and grab more attention – and sympathy – than a candle-lit vigil, or a march from A to B.

Activism is so frequently seen as dour and depressing by people who don't consider themselves political. To some, activism is synonymous with standing in the rain collecting signatures for a petition. These people yearn for something more – something they can connect with and enjoy. Give it to them. Make your protests sincerely fun, with a genuine desire to spread exuberance to passersby.

2) Intelligent media strategy

Art Uncut (an offshoot of UK Uncut, focusing specifically on cuts to the arts) wanted to highlight the legal tax avoidance of U2, an Irish band who commercially are based in the Netherlands, where

royalties on music incur almost no tax.[1] They developed an
audacious plan: storm the stage during U2's performance at
Glastonbury 2011. With such tight security this would seem
impossible. But here's the twist: if the protest never actually went
ahead, it didn't matter. The protest was an excuse to get newspapers
talking about U2 and tax avoidance. The threat of an action was
enough to get a reaction.

The plan was announced a few weeks in advance and received
huge coverage in the media. Press releases were sent out, media
contacts were informed, tweets were made, a buzz was created, and
countless people around the UK learned about U2's tax avoidance.
Even if the protest had never gone ahead, it would have been a
victory, because the message was out there. The media battle had
been won.

At the first UK Uncut protest one person was dedicated to
informing and liaising with newspapers and rolling news channels.
This helped the story to receive comprehensive, international
coverage, from Sky to Bloomberg, from *The Metro* to the *Financial
Times*.[2] Activists also made themselves available via Twitter to give
quotes and photos to news organisations. UK Uncut realised that it
is harder for the mainstream media to ignore a story if everyone is
talking about it on Twitter and Facebook. Their strong social media
presence, with useful, relevant information, had a huge impact on
how quickly the story could spread.

Soon enough, strong relationships were built and maintained
with a number of reporters from a wide range of publications.
Journalists and camera crews would frequently follow regional
groups behind the scenes. A team of people would write press
releases, and knew which news desks to send them to. The website
also gave advice on writing press releases relevant to local people,
with a focus on concentrating on local newspapers. Media expertise
was shared as widely as possible. It's always worth contacting the
local press and it's best to make your press releases as media-
friendly as possible.[3]

3) Horizontal, consensus decision making

A crucial factor in UK Uncut's success is its non-hierarchical structure, and use of consensus decision making. UK Uncut does not have a boss. Unlike most NGOs and trade union groups, there is no one team of people commanding others. Instead there is a team who facilitate administration and debate and help to put proposals into action.

In practice, nationwide protests are organised as follows: the administrators decide to call a day of action, or ask their followers on Twitter what day would be the most appropriate. They suggest a few targets, based on recently discovered tax avoiders, and start a conversation about which targets people prefer. This process elicits thousands of replies; using Twitter makes the conversation and decision making entirely transparent and democratic.

Once a decision has collectively been reached, the admins draft a press release, update the website, and create banners and leaflets that can be downloaded across the country. Of course, these resources are not obligatory, activists are encouraged to create their own protest from start to finish: design their own resources, recruit locally and handle their own press.

UK Uncut activists make things happen themselves. Knowledge is shared; responsibility is distributed. People are actively encouraged to take charge, to organise locally and to make decisions themselves. Empowering people to create a successful protest is a great motivator, and this helped to fuel the exponential growth of the movement.

Some have argued that UK Uncut is not truly non-hierarchical. Whilst, yes, the small London based team operate the website, media phone and Facebook/Twitter accounts, in terms of decision-making and direction setting, UK Uncut are worlds away from top-down organisations. Compare them to a big organisation like a union, or even the typical NGO, and you will see that they are vastly different from each other.

Even if true non-hierarchy is not suitable for your organisation or group, tools such as consensus decision making can be, and can play a significant part of how you can make individual people feel that they are a genuinely important part of your movement.[4]

4) Clear, simple, understandable messaging

Tax avoidance is a notoriously difficult concept to understand. Indeed, tax avoiders often evade detection because even the tax inspectors themselves cannot understand the complexity of the schemes that corporations and millionaires use to hide their money.

UK Uncut simplified the issue with powerful, punchy slogans. For most people, numbers like Vodafone's £6,000,000,000 tax dodge are too large to comprehend. UK Uncut solved this by telling people 'Vodafone dodged £6 billion. Coalition welfare cuts are £7 billion. If Vodafone paid their tax, disabled children could get the care they need'. Or, 'Topshop's Sir Philip Green dodged £285 million. Coalition school sports cuts are £230 million. Your kids can't play sport because Philip Green avoids tax.' When the numbers are humanised by explaining to people that Vodafone are the reason their grandparents won't receive benefits, those people won't just understand; they'll be outraged enough to join your occupation.

It's also a highly inter-generational message. In its first couple of weeks the movement consisted primarily of young people. As it spread around the country it attracted everyone from school children to the retired. The message elegantly reached across the generational divide, striking everyone's sense of compassion and fair play. We all know people who are old, who are ill, who have kids, who can't fend for themselves.

Finally, the message was upbeat. It was punctuated by a witty idea: that UK Uncut are 'Big Society Revenue and Customs'. UK Uncut took one of Cameron's key proposals, and turned it back against him. The government isn't running HMRC properly, so we'll do it for them. It comes back to the sense of fun, and offering positive solutions. UK Uncut told people 'here is an injustice; and here is how we're going to fix it'.

Put a lot of work into your message. Boil it down to something that can be explained in five seconds. Make it clear and simple, accessible and witty, and don't just criticise: offer a solution. This isn't easy, but your work will pay dividends.

5) Give people victories

Activists know there have been a great number of successful protests in recent years. Nevertheless, there is a feeling among many young people that experiences such as futile marches against the war in Iraq proved that protesting does nothing. UK Uncut is, for many young people, the first campaign group that they have actually seen work.

By interrupting trading, every UK Uncut protest is immediately successful by showing businesses that avoiding tax doesn't always pay. The importance of this simply cannot be overstated. Victory makes people happy. Constant victory inspires people to carry on.

There is also the second, long-term aim of stopping the rich from avoiding tax. There have been significant victories here. We have heard from sources within government that companies have contacted HMRC to ask how best to bring their tax in line, so that they do not become the targets of a UK Uncut action. The long term aim is audacious in its scope and moving towards it will require work from those in government, in law, in media and in corporations as well as the support of other campaigners such as the Tax Justice Network (TJN). Campaigns are often more successful when they enhance each other's work, for example the direct action of UK Uncut has highlighted the lesser known work of the TJN.

In addition, UK Uncut has scored a third victory: they have empowered people with factually accurate and devastatingly powerful arguments against the government's cuts. The issue of tax avoidance is now in the consciousness of millions – literally millions – of people who were probably unaware of the sheer scale of the issue. It is now easier to lobby political parties to make manifesto promises to close tax loopholes; but more immediately, it is now an issue that the government cannot ignore – especially when arguing that there is no alternative to the cuts. The issue of tax avoidance can be used to defeat almost any government argument in favour of austerity. You're closing libraries? Make Vodafone pay its fair share. You're privatising the NHS to save money? Make Boots pay its fair share.

Make sure all your protests have a bold but achievable goal, alongside any more audacious aspirations. Highlight your aims before the protest, and celebrate them afterwards. The victory will make you happy, it will inspire people to join in future actions, and, most importantly of all, it will have delivered immediate justice.

Notes

1. Adam Gabbatt, 'U2 Glastonbury tax protest: activists condemn "heavy-handed" security', *The Guardian*: www.guardian.co.uk/music/2011/jun/25/u2-bono-tax-protest-glastonbury.
2. See for example: Hazel Baker, 'Vodafone Shop Protest Over "Unpaid Tax Bill"', *Sky News*: http://news.sky.com/home/business/article/15777604, 2010; Duncan Robinson, 'Protestors target Vodafone over taxes': http://ft.com/cms/s/0/61f291de-e1d7-11df-b71e-00144feabdc0.html, 2011.
3. See activist-toolkit.wikispaces.com/Press+Release for a guide to writing press releases for activists.
4. See seedsforchange.org.uk/free/shortconsensus for a good introduction to consensus decision making.

Words and pictures for *The secret origin of UK uncut* by John Miers, plotting by John Miers and Chris Coltrane

John Miers has recently enrolled at St Martin's art school, where he is embarking on a crackpot scheme to earn a doctorate by making a graphic novel and writing a bunch of stuff about it. After which he will change his surname to Doom. View more of his work at www.johnmiers.com.

Chris Coltrane is a stand-up comedian, writer and activist. Alongside UK Uncut, he is involved with the skeptic, civil liberties, open internet and anti-austerity movements. He has written for sites including New Internationalist, Londonist and Liberal Conspiracy. His debut solo show, Political Policing In An Age Of Discontent, will run in London and Edinburgh during 2012.

References

Page 1

Figures for the cuts made to welfare and the NHS are taken from the 2010 governmental spending review:
http://cdn.hm-treasury.gov.uk/sr2010_completereport.pdf

Since the publication of that report, changes have been made to the funding arrangements for school sports. The quoted figure of £285m (rounded to the nearest £5m) was created by summing £125m that is no longer ring-fenced for sports in the education budget with £162m cut from school sports partnerships. Details can be found here:
www.sportdevelopment.info/index.php?option=com_
content&view=article&id=727:ruff-guide-coalition-sport-
policy&catid=54:introsv

Details of the tax arrangements of Vodafone, Boots and Sir Phillip Green are drawn from these articles:

Vodafone:
www.guardian.co.uk/commentisfree/2010/oct/22/vodafone-tax-case-
leaves-sour-taste

www.thisismoney.co.uk/money/news/article-1704527/Taxman-let-Vodafone-off-6bn-bill.html

Boots:
www.guardian.co.uk/world/2010/dec/11/boots-switzerland-uk

Sir Phillip Green:
www.guardian.co.uk/business/2005/oct/21/executivesalaries.executivepay
(this also claims that the £1.2bn bonus on which he paid no tax was the biggest pay award in corporate history)

More detail and further links regarding the above can be found at the UK Uncut website: www.ukuncut.org.uk/

Page 2

The *Financial Times* article referenced in the last panel:
www.ft.com/cms/s/0/61f291de-e1d7-11df-b71e-00144feabdc0.html

A detailed account of the day's events:
http://chris-coltrane.livejournal.com/404426.html

Page 3

The link tweeted by 'InformedObjector' in panel 3 was:
www.guardian.co.uk/business/series/tax-gap

For further details about Barclay's tax avoidance activities see:
www.independent.co.uk/news/business/news/barclays-paid-113m-tax-as-bonus-pool-was-15bn-2219279.html

Page 5

The *Daily Mail* article being read by the man in panel 3 is here:
www.dailymail.co.uk/tvshowbiz/article-2007956/U2-upstaged-tax-protest-Glastonbury-campaigners-left-deflated-security-pop-balloon.html

Details regarding Fortnum & Mason's tax avoidance can be found at:
www.taxresearch.org.uk/Blog/2011/03/28/this-is-why-uk-uncut-picked-on-fortnums/

And this provides an account of the police's treatment of the protestors:
www.guardian.co.uk/uk/2011/jul/18/fortnum-mason-uk-uncut-charges-dropped

Page 6

The *Daily Mail* article referenced in panel 2:
www.dailymail.co.uk/debate/article-2051131/The-man-taxes-belief-fair-play.html

The dialogue in panel 3 is taken verbatim from the uncorrected transcript of the questioning session:
www.tax-hell.co.uk/administration-and-effectiveness-of-hmrc-closing-the-tax-gap/

The author is obliged to make clear that at the time of writing neither witnesses nor Members have had the opportunity to correct the record. The transcript is not yet an approved formal record of these proceedings.

George Osborne's autumn statement has been widely reported; one source for the £15bn figure quoted in panel 5 is:
www.telegraph.co.uk/finance/budget/8924623/Autumn-Statement-2011-George-Osborne-introduces-six-more-years-of-pain.html

A contract between generations: pensions and saving

Craig Berry

There are few areas of social and economic life more replete with intergenerational bargains than pensions and long-term saving. Yet it cannot be denied that the intergenerational contract in policy and practice around pensions and saving has begun to unravel at a rapid rate, to the detriment of today's young people. The individualisation of the pensions system means we are not only on our own as a generation, but also within our generation.

Breach of contract

A pension is the means by which people are provided with an income in later life – when they are deemed unable to secure an income for themselves through productive activity – using funds accumulated through previous contributions to the labour market. Pension financing is always about funding one lifestage with the proceeds of another, but is not necessarily intergenerational in nature. The UK is in many ways moving towards a system whereby we finance our own retirements, from the proceeds of our own toil and investments, rather than a system whereby people of working-age fund the pension payments of the already-retired, in return for a hypothetical guarantee from future workers that they will pay for our retirements. This also means we are moving away from the kind of risk-sharing and redistributive arrangements that tend to be present in intergenerational pensions systems, therefore increasing the chances of individuals being left with little to live on in later life, if they suffer investment losses or are unable to save.

The National Insurance system is the clearest embodiment of the intergenerational contract in the UK pensions system. Of course it is little more than symbolic: state pensions are in fact paid out of general tax revenues rather than a specific National Insurance pot. However, this does not mean an intergenerational contract is not at work; ultimately, today's taxpayers are funding the state pensions of yesterday's taxpayers. However, the cumulative impact of the Thatcher government's 1980 decision to index the state pension by inflation rather than earnings has reduced the value of the intergenerational contract significantly. A large portion of the baby boom cohort opted for lower taxes instead of maintaining the value of the state pension.

The redistributive aspect of state pensions has been further undermined through the introduction of an earnings-related (not to be confused with earnings-indexed) state pension in the 1970s, enabling those who pay more tax on their income to accrue higher state pension entitlements. The Labour government sought to redress this by phasing out the earnings-related state pension top-up, and introduced the means-tested Pension Credit to lift pensioners out of poverty.

The contractual fissure is even more evident in relation to private pensions. Generous 'defined benefit' (DB) occupational pensions paid individuals a portion of their salary from retirement until death. Most schemes were unfunded, that is, financed like the state pension on a 'pay as you go' basis; within an organisation, today's workers (and their employers' profits) collectively paid the pensions of today's retirees. These schemes were only ever open to a minority of workers, although many working-class people had access through employment in the public sector or large corporations. The closure of DB schemes to new entrants is one of the defining fault lines of contemporary generational conflict, although a far wider range of factors explain the trend (and in fact, a large number of DB schemes have already become insolvent – baby boomers on the verge of retirement have been the principal victims). In the place of DB schemes have come 'defined contribution' (DC) schemes, where workers build up individual pension pots. Outcomes are not set in advance, but instead determined by investment performance, with no or minimal risk-sharing; they are also less egalitarian than salary-linked schemes, given that those able to invest higher amounts are likely to see disproportionately higher investment returns.

A rainy day

There is no alternative: we must become a generation of savers. Our reluctance to begin squirreling away every penny means we are scorned in popular culture, with even middle-class parents bemoaning their offspring's reliance on 'the bank of mum and dad'. Apparently we are ignorant of pensions and financial planning, and short-termist in outlook. The former is palpably untrue: it is natural that understanding of pensions would increase with age, and according to the Wealth and Assets Survey, twenty-five to thirty-four year olds do not understand pensions, significantly less than any other age group, especially once this lifestage effect is taken into account.[1] The irony of today's young people being depicted as short-termist, an apparent corollary of our short attention spans, is exposed by the tragedy of the 'discount rate' which allowed previous generations to effectively conceal the long-term cost of the state pension entitlements they were accruing. A lower discount rate for future liabilities means that for young people, this cover will be blown.[2]

Initiating and maintaining long-term saving depends on the availability of financial incentives. Yet young people are far less likely to be offered a pension by their employer, and those that are tend to receive lower contribution rates.[3] Pensions tax relief is only an effective incentive for the wealthiest, located in higher tax bands. Outside pensions, ISAs offer minimal tax incentives to save, which have been undermined by low Bank of England base rates. The previous government had sought to introduce 'matched' saving for the poorest families through the Saving Gateway, but plans were abandoned by the coalition government as part of fiscal consolidation.

With youth unemployment at record highs and the value of education falling, far more immediate financial priorities understandably inhibit long-term planning. Indeed, there is evidence that virtually all young households have savings of some type and that they are keen to save, albeit towards the medium term goal of getting on the housing ladder, rather than for retirement. We know that this is increasingly difficult for young people. Those that managed it before the crash saw the value of their assets rise rapidly, but they also saw mortgage debt value rise much faster than income. Affording something that our parents' generation perceived as a birthright has potentially locked young home-owners into long periods of indebtedness and financial difficulty. As such there is evidence that people are actually more likely to be contributing to a private pension in their late twenties and early thirties than their late thirties and early forties, when the pressures of family formation start to pile up.[4] Of course, the paradoxical maintenance of the intergenerational contract at the family level means that those among us from affluent families will have far less to worry about.

Another part of the explanation here is *how* we work, not simply *whether* we work. Clearly, pensions and long-term saving will always be a difficult sell when job opportunities are increasingly concentrated in temporary and unstable employment. On the other hand, many young people value the end of jobs-for-life because we want to work more flexibly and, ultimately, switch jobs or even careers frequently. We are 'job-crafters' rather than passive recipients of conventional employment roles.[5] But is pensions saving compatible with this approach to work? If not, perhaps we will have only ourselves to blame when poverty strikes in retirement. Yet Labour and Conservative governments have for decades proselytised the importance of flexibilisation to the country's economic success. The public sector boom is over, large-scale manufacturing is never coming back, and the City's house of cards has finally collapsed – it is creative and knowledge-intense service industries, where the job roles (and even the boundary between employer and employee) are evermore fluid, that will contribute most to recovery. Young people have rarely been more important economically, yet it seems we are being asked to sacrifice our long-term financial security to get Britain back on its feet.

Policy-makers have not been unconcerned by these trends, but responses have in general maintained the pensions system trajectory towards individualisation, and away from the (redistributive) intergenerational contract. The aborted Saving Gateway was part of a wider 'financial inclusion' agenda, which seems strangely ignorant of evidence that the vast majority of people will engage or have engaged with financial services at some point in their lives. The problem is not non-participation, but rather the terms upon which we are expected to participate.[6] The National Employment Savings Trust (NEST) will for the first time mandate employers to contribute to an occupational pension for their low- and middle-income employees. Individuals will be 'automatically enrolled' into a NEST account or a suitable equivalent. One of the key benefits of NEST is the portability of accounts between employers, but it offers only DC pensions, and there are justifiable concerns that low default contribution rates will mean that saving will be almost futile for low-earners in terms of the returns they can expect.

The state pension is also undergoing reform. In return for increasing the state pension age, the earnings link will be restored. The coalition government is also expected to merge the basic and earnings-related state pensions and set the new benefit at around the level that the state pension would have been, had the link not been broken in the 1980s. Baby boomers will benefit, but so too in theory will today's young people. Yet it is worth pointing out that the new state pension will be no higher than the poverty benchmark set by Pension Credit, which will now be effectively abolished. The poorest households will generally be no better off than they could have been anyway, through means-tested benefits; the main beneficiaries will be middle-income households who in the past had nominally 'lost' Pension Credit because of their income from private pensions and the earnings-related state pension.

A radical retirement

The changes initiated will do some good. It is possible that they could have gone further. NEST accounts could incorporate a cash savings pot for young members, instead or in advance of a pension saving pot, in recognition of the financial strains of early adulthood. More importantly, stronger government guarantees for NEST pots would enable risk-sharing between state and individual for low-earners, who can least afford to lose their investments (it is worth noting that DB pensions are not only better, but through the operation of the Pension Protection Fund and Financial Assistance Scheme, also better protected). The state pension could be higher still, or perhaps more innovatively, could include a premium for those with lower life expectancy who are less likely to get their fair share. Revisiting the idea of matched saving, targeted at young people, would also be welcome.

These relatively minor reforms would help to encourage saving and enable fairer pensions outcomes. But a more radical rethink of policy in this area may be required. The traditional format of pension contributions deducted from earnings may remain appropriate to some extent, but it seems logical that capital accumulated through various means should be part of a fiscal and regulatory framework that is broadly equivalent to pensions. It should be easier for low-income households to convert property wealth and ordinary savings, for instance, into a retirement income, and the state must play a role in designing and protecting the financial instruments that will be required in this regard.

Moreover, because it is ultimately employment in this earlier period that will enable private pensions saving, there must be a greater distribution of decent employment opportunities for young people. We may be able to accept the individualisation of pensions, assuming we are equipped with the capabilities to make provision for ourselves – especially the most disadvantaged young people, whose retirement outcomes will reflect cumulative disadvantage over the lifecourse. The cradle-to-grave welfare settlement may be gone, never to return, but the state must reorient itself towards supporting individuals at key lifestages, such as the transition into adulthood, and then into retirement.

Finally, if young people are to accept that we must engage intimately with financial services in order to secure a retirement income, genuine financial citizenship must become a reality.[7] The vast majority of us are already financially included, now we need to be financially empowered. At the micro level this means having much greater say over how our pensions saving is invested, which is actually far more feasible now that most of us will have individual rather than collective pots. At the macro level this means the financial system must be placed under much greater scrutiny and held accountable by public authorities with a democratic mandate. We cannot be expected to trust our futures to a system over which we have little control.

Craig Berry is a Senior Researcher at the International Longevity Centre-UK and former Policy Advisor on Older People and State Pensions at HM Treasury. He also lectures on economic policy at the University of Warwick. He completed his PhD, on globalisation and UK trade policy, at the University of Sheffield in 2008, and his book *Globalisation and Ideology in Britain: Neoliberalism, Free Trade and the Global Economy* was published by Manchester University Press in 2011.

Notes

1. Office for National Statistics, 'Wealth in Great Britain', ONS website: search for 'wealth survey 2006' and click through the top result.
2. Angus Hanton, 'Discount Rate: A Small Number with Surprisingly Large

Consequences', Intergenerational Foundation website: www.if.org.uk/archives/19/discount-rate, 2011.

3. Craig Berry, 'Resuscitating Retirement Saving', International Longevity Centre-UK website: www.ilcuk.org.uk/files/pdf_pdf_178.pdf, 2011.

4. Richard Boreham & James Lloyd, 'Asset Accumulation Across the Lifecourse', International Longevity Centre-UK website: www.ilcuk.org.uk/files/pdf_pdf_32.pdf, 2007.'

5. Hae Jung Kim et al, 'Generation Y Employees Retail Work Experience: The Mediating Effect of Job Characteristics', *Journal of Business Research*, 2009, p62.

6. Jane Midgley, 'Financial Inclusion, Universal Banking and Post Offices in Britain', *Area* 37(3) 2005.

7. Craig Berry, *Financial Citizenship: The State's Role in Enabling Individuals to Save*, Friends Provident Foundation 2011.

'Overqualified and underemployed': young people, education and the economy

Martin Allen and Patrick Ainley

In the last two decades, staying on in full-time education post-16 has become the norm, with more than 8 out of 10 in the age group continuing in school or college. Indeed, some kind of training or 'learning' will become compulsory up to the age of 17 in 2013 and 18 in 2015. As a consequence, rates of attainment in public examinations have reached levels previously inconceivable. As late as the 1970s, up to 40 per cent of youngsters left school without any qualifications, and most of them found jobs without any of the 'vocational preparation' now deemed necessary. Today, over 70 per cent of 16 year olds attain 5 A*-C grades GCSE, with the numbers awarded top grades increasing every year since the exam was introduced in the 1980s.

Once a 'gold standard' qualification for a small minority, A-levels have become a mass qualification (and students still tend to opt for either the arts or the sciences). New courses in new subjects have been introduced, and there are now approaching one million entries each year, with A/A* grades awarded to 1 in 4 candidates. A succession of 'alternative' vocational courses has also been also introduced, but most young people who have a choice have preferred A-levels; New Labour's specialist diploma was an expensive failure.

As to Higher Education students – only 2 per cent (mostly men) were educated at this level after the war, but by the time New Labour left office, over 40 per cent of young people were entering some form of higher education, and the proportion of female students (57 per cent of undergraduates) has now surpassed that of males, with 42 per cent of all 18-21 year old men in HE compared with 47 per cent of 18-21 year old women. Before the current government came to office, successive previous governments had encouraged staying on in higher education, arguing that the changing economy demanded highly skilled professional and managerial jobs, whilst demand for unskilled work was declining. Governments also promoted a lifelong-learning culture, with training and retraining provided for an increasingly flexible workforce in order to keep up with technological change. This was supposed to provide opportunities for general upward social mobility.

As a result, the current generation of young people have become the most highly qualified ever, even if a small but significant minority still leave the education system with very little. But in spite of this, this generation is likely to be the first to end up with lower standards of living than their parents.[1] Our aim here is to question commonly held assumptions about education, and to argue for a more comprehensive set of policies for young people – since we cannot educate our way out of recession.

Whatever happened to social mobility? The class structure goes pear-shaped

First, we question the role that endless cramming for more qualifications can play in promoting individual advancement in what has become a new religion of salvation through education. Rather than education promoting opportunities, the system increasingly ensures that everyone remains in their place. This is in contrast to the post-war period, when relatively large numbers of working-class school-leavers moved into 'middle-class' jobs. This increased social mobility was made possible because – with economic growth and expansion of the welfare state – the total number of such jobs increased. But this period of limited upward social mobility came to an end from 1965 on, in spite of the expansion of Higher Education as recommended by Robbins in 1963. (Though this coincided with the introduction of comprehensive schools, it was not a consequence of it.[2])

Children born from the mid-1970s onwards have therefore experienced a decline in the opportunities for absolute upward mobility. This is because, despite some increase in managerial and professional jobs, there are nowhere near enough to meet the aspirations of all those who want them, while many occupations that now call themselves 'professional' are more accurately described as 'para-professional'. Meanwhile, at the bottom of the occupational structure, 'Mcjobs' continue to expand, so that 40 per cent of all jobs in Britain now require only one or two days experience for most people to perform effectively.

This has led some commentators, such as Hutton 1995, to argue that occupational structure is like an hour-glass.[3] We would argue that it is more accurate to see it as pear–shaped, because, while unskilled, casualised employment is growing at the base of the old social pyramid, many 'professional or managerial' occupations are being proletarianised towards the level of waged labour, with the loss of former autonomy and security. The same processes of deskilling that devastated the skilled and 'respectable' manual working class with the dismantling of apprenticeships for heavy industry in the 1970s are now reaching up the employment hierarchy.[4] This leaves many in the 'squeezed middle'/working class trying to run up a down-escalator of deflating qualifications, so as not to fall into the worthlessly certified 'new rough', so-called 'underclass' beneath.

Central to this has been the way in which new information and communications technology has been used to automate, deskill, downsize and contract out. These processes have been applied to many traditionally middle-class occupations, breaking them down into 'bite-size chunks' for measurement, to meet new managerial targets. This creates sub-occupations that can be carried out by 'para-professionals' – for example classroom and care assistants, community police officers and many para-medical roles, and also various kinds of private sector sales-persons.

So, is youth unemployment a skills problem? Young people and the jobs queue

The second assumption we want to challenge is related to the first, but deserves separate attention because it is embedded in educational literature – namely, that increased participation in education is the result of increased technical and intellectual demands in the workplace, a rise in what Marx (with reference to the move to industry from 'the idiocy of rural life') called 'the general intellect'. Despite increases in the general level of education – or certification, at least – almost 1 million 16-24 year olds are officially unemployed, while many more have given up looking for work and are 'economically inactive'.

Un- and under-employment also increasingly affects graduates, and there has been a graduatisation of a swathe of office and retail occupations. 'Top jobs' are reserved for graduates from 'top universities' – though even this is not guaranteed, when there were 80 applications for each post according to the Association of Graduate Recruiters in 2011. Of other employers, 4 out of 5 only recruit those with 1sts or 2.1s, so that towards the end of 2010, the Office for National Statistics reported the unemployment rate for new graduates to be 20 per cent. Of those in employment, over a third are not in 'graduate jobs', and starting salaries below £15,000 are not uncommon. Unpaid 'internships' are the graduate equivalent of 'work experience' for school leavers, or 'apprenticeships without jobs' in FE.

Of course, this doesn't mean that some employers do not really need people with particular qualifications to fill vacancies, and will give them preference, but the labour market is more like a 'jobs queue' – the more qualifications a young person has, the further up the queue they are likely to be. In this respect, those without qualifications are four times as likely to be unemployed as those with degrees; while those with only GCSEs are half as likely. The differential, however, is a consequence of the level of qualifications held by others in the queue, rather than economic demand.

So, instead of educational qualifications lifting people up the occupational structure, more and more young people pursue educational qualifications to protect themselves from 'sliding down' into a 'new rough' section of the formerly manually working class, which has been relegated to so-called 'underclass' status. The grandchildren of the YTS generation are increasingly disconnected from society and without hope – they are the group represented by the summer rioters. This group is growing in number, and of course includes many who did not and would not participate in these activities.

This can be seen as a reconstitution of what Marx called the 'Reserve Army of Labour' (i.e. the use of mass unemployment in order to drive down wages and conditions for those in work) – something that Gamble sees as being 'One of the key functions of economic crisis'.[5] But this latest reconstitution takes a new form: the lives of millions are wasted not only by long-term unemployment, but, increasingly, by festering in insecure, part-time work, interspersed with, and often concomitant with, warehousing in sixth forms, college and university. Youth is thus 'wasted' in several senses at once.[6]

The Coalition can only make things worse

In response to this growing generational crisis for young people – and therefore for society as a whole – the Tories have launched an offensive against education. Exploiting the contradictions of New Labour's 'standards agenda' in schools, Education minister Michael Gove is bent on restoring traditional 'grammar school' approaches to learning, denouncing the growth of 'soft' subjects and pledging to end 'the culture of modules and re-sits'. Following the riots, Cameron has also emphasised restoring 'discipline in the classroom'. This is part of a general social programme designed to police and control youth.

Gove and universities minister David Willets plainly consider that too many working-class kids have gone to universities, and by allowing tuition fees to triple are attempting to price them out of higher education. As an alternative, they promise 'apprenticeships', when it's perfectly clear that, despite being offered subsidies, most employers don't need apprentices, and if they do they train them themselves. Thus, with a few exceptions, such as BT and Rolls Royce, which are reported to be harder to get into than Oxford, the majority of apprenticeships that do exist will be nothing more than 'apprenticeships without jobs'. Provided by colleges or private training organisations only able to simulate the experiences of the workplace, these will predictably resemble the failed youth training schemes of the 1980s, which were branded *Training Without Jobs* by Finn in 1987.[7]

The strongest argument against fees and for EMAs therefore remains – what else are all these young people supposed to do?

Real alternatives are needed

Despite the dominating role it plays in their lives, we have moved beyond the period when education appeared to be the most important determinant of young people's futures. In all European countries – even Finland, where the education system is often used as a shining example of how things could be – youth unemployment rates are high. Whilst in the past the English education system, without any republican notion of entitlement to education, failed the majority by selecting only a minority at each stage to go on to the next, today it is the economy that is failing the education system. Of course, we need to campaign for the restoration of EMAs and for free HE for all those who want it, but what's needed more is an employment strategy that goes beyond the supply side of education and training.

Specific policies for youth are needed *in addition* to a wider programme to restore prosperity and mitigate climate change with *A Million Green Jobs Now*.[8] Despite its limitations, Labour's Future Jobs Fund, which offered subsidies to employers to recruit unemployed youth, was a step in the right direction. Though only providing short-term placements on the minimum wage, it was at least an acknowledgement that it is no good improving young people's skills and qualifications if there are no jobs to apply for.

We must go much further however. All employers should have incentives to employ local young people. Local authority, public sector and voluntary sector organisations, in particular, must play a major part in generating employment opportunities – for example, by introducing quotas for employing young people. Local authorities and their partner organisations can also play a key role in generating apprenticeships that provide guaranteed jobs for those who complete them. There also needs to be a specific housing policy for young people for the first time, going beyond foyers and student hostels.[9]

But our central concern in this contribution is with education, and here a new role for schools, colleges, universities and adult education is called for, as centres for recreation and regeneration. This presents huge challenges for teachers and their unions, because they remain wedded to the post-war 'partnership' model, where teachers work with governments to achieve shared social and economic objectives, and in return enjoy the status of 'professionals', for whom interest in young people is restricted to what happens in the classroom. As Roberts remarks, 'the ending of the link between education and employment and the collapse of any real opportunities for social mobility presents huge challenges for them', as well as for a wider progressive politics, given that the old nostrums no longer apply: 'expand GDP and become better educated, trained and qualified'.[10] Instead, as we argue in *New Strategies for Youth and Education*, we must develop new unity and understanding between generations, as well as overcoming divisions within them.[11]

Patrick Ainley is Professor of Training and Education at the University of Greenwich School of Education and Training (as was). Books include: *Learning Policy, Towards the Certified Society*, Macmillan 1999; *Apprenticeship: Towards a New Paradigm of Learning* (edited with Helen Rainbird) Kogan Page 1999; *The Business of Learning, Staff and Student Experiences of Further Education in the 1990s* (with Bill Bailey), Cassell 1997; *Degrees of Difference, Higher Education in the 1990s*, Lawrence and Wishart 1994; *Class and Skill*, Cassell 1993; *Training for the Future, The rise and fall of the Manpower Services Commission* (with Mark Corney), Cassell 1990; *From School to YTS*, Open University Press 1988. You can find him on Facebook and/or follow him on Twitter as Ollover Krumwall.

Martin Allen is a researcher and a part-time economics teacher in a west London sixth form. He completed a PhD thesis at the Open University (2004) on the changing relationship between young people, work and vocational qualifications. He was Vice Chair of National Union of Teachers Secondary Advisory Committee between 2002-2011 and has been a union activist since 1985.

Patrick and Martin are joint authors of *Education Make You Fick, Innit?* Tufnell Press 2007; and *Lost Generation? New strategies for youth and education*, Continuum 2010. They blog at http://radicaled. wordpress.com/.

Notes

1. K. Roberts, 'The end of the long baby-boomer generation? If so what next?', Unpublished draft paper 2010.
2. S. Aronowitz, *Against Schooling, For an education that matters*, Paradigm 2008.

3. W. Hutton, *The State We're In*, Jonathan Cape 1995.

4. H. Braverman, *Labor and Monopoly Capital*, Monthly Review Press 1974.

5. A. Gamble, *The Spectre at the Feast*, Palgrave Macmillan 2009, p47.

6. M. Cheeseman, *The pleasures of being a student at the University of Sheffield*, University of Sheffield, unpublished PhD thesis 2011.

7. D. Finn, *Training without Jobs, New Deals and Broken Promises*, Macmillan 1987.

8. Campaign Against Climate Change, *One Million Climate Jobs Now*, CACC 2010.

9. G. Jones, *Youth*, Polity 2009.

10. K. Roberts, *The end of the long baby-boomer generation? If so what next?*, Unpublished draft paper 2010.

11. P. Ainley and M. Allen, *Lost Generation? New Strategies for Youth and Education*, Continuum 2010.

Radical learning and learning to be a bit radical

Jamie Audsley and Jim O'Connell

After working in youth work, teaching and community organising, Jamie and Jim imagine a radical day at school, based on the principles of trusting people to organise, mutuality and solidarity, through the eyes of Josie, a 15-year-old living on the outskirts of her city.

Josie goes to the Hardie-Webb Community School, one of the expanding members of the Co-operative School Network. This is a Tuesday morning in October, and with the abolition of OFSTED, she's been asked to keep a diary to help review her school and assess its progress.

7.10am: My alarm clock goes. I thump it and slump out of bed. After a shower and saying goodbye to Mum I walk to school. Dad's at work already but he's coming to school to do a workshop about developing youth leadership in our area. The walk to school takes 20 minutes. Our neighbourhood got pretty badly damaged in the 2011 riots, but when we got a new headteacher she made us change to a co-operative school and join this thing called the CitySafe Scheme. Now I'm a Year 11 I'm a CitySafe Captain, and my job is to look out for shopkeepers and other people in the area, and they also look out for us. It's much safer than when I was younger, and nice to know more people. When I'm walking to school I use my ipad and online organising stuff to find where my friends are and catch up with them. Then George, who is the school community organiser, comes up to us. He says that the council is re-planning the high street and Year 9 are helping for

Geography and Craft, Design and Technology. They're doing an assembly to Year 7s in the visual learning centre to make them get involved too.

8am: When I got to school I went to cook an omelette for breakfast with Sally, who is one of my mum's best friends. I sit facing the shiny new school crest in the canteen. Our motto bounces out at me: 'Achieving Freedom and Excellence for all through Cooperation'. And beneath it, 'Raising everyone's abilities and aptitudes through hard work, a focus on our talents and learning to create change with our community'. I didn't fully understand what it meant when I started here; I get it now, but still think it's a bit over the top. What's wrong with 'we're better, together' or something like that?

8.15am: I head to see my tutor Miss Hall to get some advice on doing the school assessment. She's awesome; she's like a couple of the other new teachers, really easy to get along with. Mum says it's because she did her training with loads of other kinds of professionals: youth workers, social workers and community organisers. So she knows lots more than just school stuff and really helps if there's ever a problem. She reminds me of the success criteria students, teachers, governors, parents and some man from government worked with us to agree. Basically, we need to learn how 'to be the change we want to see in the world' as well as getting involved with the local community, developing our own special talents and trying to be really healthy. All this on top of GCSEs!

8.30am: Lesson 1 is Human Geography. Our teacher Mr Jones says it's all about people and the places they live in, so we're already experts because we're people who can think about the places we live in.

Mr Jones does his lessons in two parts this year – he calls it the 'Facts' half and the 'Thinking' half. He decided to do this after the meeting with us, our parents and the governors on the first day of term. They figured there's a whole bunch of stuff we have to know for our GCSEs, so we should make sure we know it all so the man from the government can be happy. So that's why we start with Facts. Can be a bit boring though. There's a Thinking bit because finally they decided that just knowing stuff wouldn't be that useful for us in life. So Mr Jones says we have to apply what we've learned to our own lives and what we think of our area. He sets us a different thinking challenge every week. Some of them are really hard. Once a term he gets one of the planning people from the Council to come in and tell us what they would do for the challenge.

9.30am: English. Boring. The grown-ups all decided we have to do Shakespeare. I said we should act things out more but they said we should wait and see if that was worth doing – one of the governors is watching how it works at the MacDonald Academy (I think the Prime Minister had had too many chicken nuggets when he let them set it up), where they've done acting in English for 3 years now. I just think it would be more fun if we weren't just reading it all the time.

10.30am: Break.

10.45am: Science. We're getting a master-class from some business that makes Semiconductors outside the ring road. They're talking us through how they stamp silicon into computer chips. They want us to measure something called 'the differing conductivity' of some mineral they're experimenting with, at different thicknesses. Dad says they're using us for cheap labour but my friend Sally who loves technology is really into it. Says it'll look good on her UCAS form.

11.45am: Life skills class. Our teacher, Ms Malone, is a bit weird. Actually this whole thing is a bit weird. We have this lesson once a fortnight. Today, we're being taken to a bank in town. We're going to a reception for local business directors. Before we go Ms Malone tells us what we have to say and do – basically, we just have to memorise a list of talking points and chit chat to the men in suits. We also have to do things like making eye contact and laughing in the right places, which I'm not very good at, but I'm getting better. There's food, so most of us spend most of the time by the sandwich table. My mum thinks this is a load of rubbish but my dad says he would have found it really useful if someone had given him this kind opportunity before he left school.

1pm: Lunch. I eat outside with my friends. At lunchtime people from the National Volunteer Service based in the school are around. They're 19 and have been doing it for a year. One of them, Tayyiba, was telling me how she was working in her mosque to get mothers talking about opportunities for their daughters. She also tells me that Shelter's local Housing Hub are coming to school soon to run a session to teach people how we can better use the space in our houses and build better storage. I'll get Dad to do that! I like them because when my friend Emily's dad got fired from his job, they employed him, and he says it's better than his old job anyway. When I do National Service stuff I want to start a school paper working with students across the community to get our views across, I think I want to be a journalist when I'm older!

After lunch I take a walk to the community services part of the school which everyone locally has access to. There's an old people's home, a shuttle bus to the local university and my older sister is doing an apprenticeship with one of the local businesses who have some office space here. I head to the 'Knowledge Hub', which is basically a kind of cool library, but one where you can talk and work, and people have meetings there. Other people from youth clubs and places like that come in to work there too. I need to speak with Mr Boyce, the librarian and retired teacher, about what history sources I can find for my next lesson. He's helpful and he also tells me about ideas he's putting to the school meeting tonight – stuff about weaving the curriculum, culture and community even closer together.

1.45pm: History. History is fun. Today we're learning about World War 2 again. But, we're also learning about why it was important to fight fascism and what we created after the war. The parents and teachers decided we should do it this way. There was a bit of a storm, and some people thought we were doing too much politics and not enough history. I like learning the whole story though. I think it's important to think about the consequences and how it changed how we treat people. We started doing things differently to how we had done them before. We made sure everyone and all the returning soldiers had a job. We made sure you didn't have to pay to go to the doctor or for hospital any more with the NHS. We said that if you went unemployed, you could have benefits.

2.30pm: French. They tried to make French fun, but it's not. They said it was important but it is, and always will be, boring. Especially period 6. I'm quite good at it though.

3.30pm: End of lessons. I have netball practice after school. I like netball and I get into the team most weeks. We play on Saturdays and loads of local people come to watch – it's so much more fun than when it was just us. Since they made sport compulsory to pass Year 11, loads more people have been playing too. I don't know if it's good for everyone, but it's great for me.

4.30pm: Open learning club if we want to go. The Year 11s say it's useful for helping them do their work to pass their exams. I often use it to go see my tutor and discuss my talent plan: who I am, what I'm aiming for, how will I contribute – like how I'm progressing with software to create a CitySafe phone app for the local shops to get the latest updates. Today I pop in to blog the next steps the school council is taking and I update my careers interest blog too, so

Miss Hall can think about how she can support me and my writing. I also catch a team working on planning the planting for our outdoor learning space.

5pm: Home! It's been a long day …

7.30pm: Back at School. Not sure how I managed that. There's a meeting about how the school is run that mum wanted to come along to. Basically the school has a big list of values that guide how it all works and what we have to do. The values get decided in big workshops and meetings with all the parents, teachers, kids, the head teacher and some local people, like business people and church and mosque leaders. Tonight someone is proposing that we add 'discipline' to our list of values. We already have 'competitiveness', 'work', 'creativity', 'patriotism', 'inclusion' and 'respect'. There have been some behaviour issues at the start of the year, and some parents want to change our values so we can change the rules and make things tougher.

Mr Jones says he's got everything under control. That's good enough for some people but not for others. One of the church leaders suggests taking the trouble-makers and getting them mentored in the church, with a few of the local volunteers. Most people think this is a good plan.

8.30pm: Home – again. I've been thinking today that I like my school on the whole – sometimes it's boring, sometimes it's weird and sometimes it's hard. But what I like is that everyone wants us to do well. And, if it looks like a group of people isn't doing so well everyone works together to change things so there's an opportunity for them. Of course, we all have to work hard to make the most of ourselves, but there's a real sense that we're all in it together and the whole school won't let us down. People learn, work and live close to each other.

Jamie Audsley is currently undertaking a Clore Social Fellowship, a leadership programme that identifies, connects and develops aspiring leaders in the third sector. After working as a researcher at The Young Foundation on democracy and social innovation projects, he went on to become a project coordinator at London Youth, and undertook the Teach First programme to spend two years as a Geography and Science teacher. He joined Citizens UK in 2009 as a community organiser with special responsibility for schools, work involving the development of leaders in civil society and the integration of community organising into the education sector.

Jim O'Connell is a teacher and is currently working as the Vice President (Graduates) at Oxford University Student's Union. He trained at schools in Reading and Chipping Norton and has previously taught financial literacy in London. He has undergone community organising training and taught financial literacy as part of a project run by London Citizens; he has also volunteered with Movement for Change.

Don't tell me the sky's the limit: social enterprise and the not-for-profit economy

David Floyd

> Don't tell me the sky's the limit, when there are footprints on the moon.
>
> Melody Hossaini

This is the verdict of Melody Hossaini, 26-year-old *Apprentice* candidate, and as a result one of the UK's best-known social entrepreneurs. While Hossaini's social enterprise youth consultancy business, InspirEngage, may have a fairly limited impact on the social, political and economic life of the UK, her emergence on the nation's favourite business talent show marks the latest step in the growth of social enterprise as a phenomenon.

In 2002, a social enterprise was defined by the then Department of Trade and Industry as: 'a business with primarily social objectives whose surpluses are principally reinvested for that purpose in the business or in the community, rather than being driven by the need to maximise profit for shareholders and owners'. While debates about whether this definition is correct (and, if so, what it means) are passionate and long-running, conceptual confusion has done little to inhibit the growth of the social enterprise movement.

For those of us born since 1979, the emergence of social enterprise has helped to fill a gap left by steady decline of the traditional co-operative movement (perhaps now beginning to enjoy a marginal recovery) and a crisis of faith in the public sector as a vehicle for positive social change.

While the popularisation of social enterprise provokes as many

163

big questions as it answers – not least for those directly involved –
what it definitely does offer is a space to deliver goods and services
using economic approaches with aims that extend beyond the
maximisation of private profit.

A growing phenomenon

Having first been strongly promoted in the mid-1990s – most
notably in Blairite thinker Charles Leadbeater's influential 1997
Demos publication, *The Rise of the Social Entrepreneur* – social
enterprise is now growing fast in the UK.

It's growing fast from a relatively small base. *Fightback Britain*, a
recent report published by Social Enterprise UK(SEUK), the
national umbrella body for UK social enterprise, revealed that:

> Across Britain, 1 in 7 of all social enterprises is a start-up, more
> than three times the proportion of start-ups in mainstream small
> businesses (14% compared to 4%). London is home to an even
> greater number, where 1 in 5 social enterprises is a start-up.
> There are an estimated 62,000 social enterprises in the UK.

Added to the fact that the number of social enterprises is increasing,
social enterprises are also more likely to be increasing their turnover
than conventional small businesses. The research shows that: '58%
of social enterprises grew last year compared to 28% of Small and
Medium-sized Enterprises (SMEs). And 57% of social enterprises
are predicting growth in the next 12 months, in comparison to 41%
of SMEs.'

Unlike conventional small businesses, social enterprises are
disproportionately likely to be situated in deprived communities
with: '39% of all social enterprises are based and working in the
most deprived communities in the UK, compared to 13% of all
SMEs. A third of all social enterprise start-ups have originated in
the UK's poorest areas ...'

And, importantly for the post-1979 generation, the range of people leading social enterprises is more diverse than within the conventional business community. According to the *Fightback Britain* report, amongst social enterprises there are 86 per cent that boast at least one female director: 'Further, 27% of leadership teams have directors from black and minority ethnic groups and 7% have directors under the age of 24. In comparison, just 13% of the Institute of Directors' membership is female and only 1% of its members are 29 years or under.'

None of this is to suggest that social enterprise is poised to take over the UK economy. Depending on which flagship social enterprises are or aren't included in overall turnover figures, the most that organisations widely regarded as social enterprises are estimated to generate is between 1 per cent and 2 per cent of GDP, but thousands of people are starting social enterprises every year, and those people are more likely to be young and living in deprived areas.

Traditional values in a modern context

While most prominent organisations involved in social enterprise, such as the first regional social enterprise development agency, Social Enterprise London, have emerged from the traditional co-operative movement, the rise of the social enterprise brand could be seen as a symptom of that movement's failure to respond to the dawn of neoliberalism.

Whether or not those of us born since 1979 know the history of the Rochdale Pioneers, none of us are able to remember the time (less than fifty years ago) when the Co-Operative was Britain's leading general store (they didn't have supermarkets then in the way we have them now). And those few of us who've read about Tony Benn's 1970s championing of worker-controlled motorbike factories are likely to place the idea somewhere on the spectrum between quaint and ridiculous. We never had the chance to vote for or against Mrs Thatcher, or (in most cases) John Major, but most of us have at least implicitly accepted the notion that businesses are owned by business people who pay us wages and generate profits for themselves.

Most co-operatives in the UK are happy to operate – to a lesser or greater extent – under the broader banner of social enterprise, but the social enterprise movement as a whole is not inherently interested in pursuing the goal of an increase in collective economic power, or in ensuring that businesses are run in accordance with particular democratic principles.

Social enterprise, as the DTI definition shows, is more about what organisations do (for customers and people who use their services) than what they are. This has a number of implications. One is to make the idea of social enterprise more easily accessible to those of us who have grown up in era when solidarity and collective decision-making was, at best, out of fashion. Another is to make social enterprises difficult to define with clarity, and (partly as a consequence) extremely useful to politicians.

Exciting, expedient and conceptually elastic

In the UK, social enterprise emerged as a quintessentially Blairite phenomenon. Dr Simon Teasdale of the Third Sector Research Centre explains that: 'To some extent social enterprises, which appeared to marry economic and social goals, were an organisational exemplar of the third way.'

Having ditched the idea of (deliberately) reducing the size of private sector (relative to the public sector) or even making serious attempts to regulate its activities, New Labour thinkers eagerly latched on to the idea that positive social change could and should be delivered directly through the free market. In fact, through social enterprise, the innovative approaches prevalent in the private sector could be harnessed to transform the delivery of publicly funded services. As Charles Leadbeater explained in *The Rise of the Social Entrepreneur*: 'A modern mobile society will only cohere if we are prepared to innovate with new ways of delivering welfare. That is what social entrepreneurs do. That is why they are so important.'

One of the most prominent examples of New Labour support for social enterprises in public service delivery was the Department of Health's Right to Request scheme, launched in mid-2008, a year after Tony Blair's departure. As outlined on the Department's website: 'Right to Request entitled clinical staff to request to deliver their services through a social enterprise. Staff had the right to put forward a social enterprise proposal to their PCT board, and to have this proposal considered. PCTs were obliged to consider these applications and, if a proposal was approved, to support the development of that social enterprise.' While the uptake of this opportunity was relatively limited (around thirty social enterprises, mostly fairly small, had spun out of the NHS under the scheme by the time it was closed in September 2010), Right to Request pointed the direction of travel for an incoming Coalition government keen to champion the idea of social enterprise 'mutuals' in theory (if not necessarily in practice).

Beyond 'idealism vs. pragmatism'

While social enterprise in the UK had until 2007 been primarily been championed as an exciting and innovative way to make public service delivery better and (hopefully) cheaper, the collapse of the global economy challenged the prevailing orthodoxy that private sector business was rolling along fine. This has opened up an opportunity for the social enterprise movement to rediscover its co-operative routes, and to combine its public service delivery role with an alternative approach to doing mainstream business.

As yet, this change in the landscape has not resulted in the emergence of major new social enterprise initiatives in the mainstream market economy. Rather, it has led to a minor revival in the fortunes of existing major players such as the Co-operative Group and the employee-owned John Lewis Partnership – and an increase in the extent to which those organisations emphasise their social values in their marketing (e.g. The Co-op's recent 'Join the Revolution' advertising campaign). However the majority of people active within the social enterprise movement, as well as those looking to start social enterprises, operate (or aspire to operate) on a far smaller scale.

Many of the younger people starting social enterprises are making a decision to do so after an experience of – or as an alternative to – working in the public sector. For, while the public sector ethos remains intact, if under heavy strain, in professions that involve direct and widely appreciated work with people – such as teaching or nursing – there is less scope for job satisfaction for those working in, say, a benefits office or local authority housing department. Here you are likely to be both hated and powerless to help.

While it may or may not have been neoliberal ideology that broke the public sector, many idealistic younger people see little hope of rebuilding it from the inside. For those who've had a taste of life working for the council or the NHS in an office role, working for or starting a social enterprise offers an opportunity for a counter-attack against the uninspiring siege mentality of the organisations they have left behind.

Though many organisations started by younger social entrepreneurs may be fuelled by a pragmatic idealism similar to that which motivated the early co-operators or those that build the post-1945 welfare state, few of them are set up with the intention of collectively distributing power and profit, or delivering universal public services.

Younger social entrepreneurs are more like to launch innovative small businesses designed to tackle specific social problems. Two recent examples are Tokunbo Ajasa Oluwa's Catch 22 – a social enterprise media company that works with industry giants to provide opportunities for young adults to break into journalism and other creative industries – and Red Button Design – formed by Amanda Jones and James Brown to manufacture the Midomo, a sustaining product to provide access to clean drinking water (as featured on *Dragons' Den*).

A space worth occupying

Some regard social enterprise as a noun – a type of organisation, however loosely defined. Others regard it as a verb – the activity of delivering (or seeking to deliver) positive social change based on some form of business principles.

It's not necessary to fully resolve this tension in order to accept and embrace the existence of a growing social enterprise movement in the UK. That movement definitely does exist, and it's a space where large numbers of people are coming together to seek solutions to social problems – either to specific problems or as a response to the wider challenge of doing business in an economically and environmentally sustainable way.

While the Thatcher government and those that followed, at least implicitly, lionised entrepreneurs as creators of as much monetary wealth as possible with limited regard for the consequences – social enterprise seeks to harness the can-do spirit of the entrepreneur to deliver wider social goods. For the post-1979 generation, the fact that social enterprise is a space to be shaped, as opposed to an existing defined structure with rules and procedures to be signed up to, makes it accessible and potentially exciting.

Different social entrepreneurs take social enterprise in different directions, and not all socially enterprising activities necessarily fit neatly under the banner of left-of-centre political thinking. What matters is the principle that individuals and groups can come together to deliver the blend of idealism, pragmatism and hard work that can make good things happen.

David Floyd is Managing Director of the social enterprise Social Spider CIC, and co-author of *Better Mental Health in a Bigger Society* (Mental Health Providers Forum). He is a trustee of Voluntary Action Waltham Forest and Urban Forum, and a fellow of the School for Social Entrepreneurs and the RSA. He is a member of the Council of Social Enterprise UK.

Beyond saving the NHS: the future of our health

Guppi Bola and Christo Albor

'Of all forms of inequality, injustice in health is the most shocking and most inhumane.' So said Martin Luther King Jr, in 1966.[1] His words continue to resonate today. In our work, the two of us have come to the conclusion that health inequality is a problem that our generation in particular is faced with. One of us, as a social epidemiologist, has spent four years researching health inequalities in the UK. The other, as a health activist, has spent the same amount of time campaigning for equal access to healthcare world-wide. Together, we think that the political focus on health should be to diminish inequalities in health, and to develop a healthcare system that promotes equality. We believe strongly that, with respect to health, these are the two priorities that our generation should collectively mobilise around. In this chapter we explain why health inequalities and ill-designed health systems are our problems, and we suggest some solutions to them.

Why is it wrong that, today, the poorer you are the sooner you will die?

In the 1930s, men in 'unskilled' occupations were about 35 per cent less likely to reach the age of 65 than men in 'professional' occupations.[2] Socioeconomic inequality in health has been a reality as long as health records were collected in the UK, and it still exists today. Poor people died younger in the 1930s mainly because of the physical strain and accidents from manual labour, deficiencies in the diet afforded by low incomes, and the spread of infection in overcrowded homes. These are not the reasons why poor people die younger in 2011. Today, service jobs that have almost entirely replaced manual labour are much less risky, low incomes can now stretch to afford healthy groceries, and the problem of overcrowding has been greatly reduced since the clearance of slums.

Yet health inequalities remain. It is likely that a major reason for the continuing expectation of incrementally shorter lives for people in every lower band of income amongst our generation is people's differing psychological experiences of life. In other words, the poorer you are and the less respected your profession is, the more persistently you will find yourself in a mentally stressed state throughout your life. Indeed, studies of professional and social hierarchies amongst people have consistently found that stress is more chronic and more pathological for every rung lower down the hierarchy.[3] Now, although the majority of people do not think that lifelong stress leads to a shorter life expectancy, both laboratory and population studies of stress hormones, most famously cortisol, have found clear associations between stress overload and physical illnesses related to the heart and to metabolism.[4]

On top of this, currently, poorer people who live fewer years spend more of their last years of life with a disability. Extrapolating from this for our generation, those of us who will have shorter lives are likely to also endure a longer period of suffering before they die. So health inequality is not simply a matter of longevity. Today's socioeconomic health inequalities reflect both the unequal experience of psychological wellbeing throughout the course of people's lives, and the unequal distribution of suffering at the end of people's lives.

Reducing health inequalities

It is always easier to isolate what is wrong than to identify the right way to solve a problem. With respect to health inequalities, potential solutions have rarely been evaluated. This is because the proposed solutions lie beyond the usual scope of healthcare politics – such as the structure of the National Health Service – and are often deeply interwoven with many other areas of policy. As Michael Marmot, author of the Strategic Review of Health Inequalities post-2010, wrote: 'Action on health inequalities requires action across all the social determinants of health'.[5] The 'social determinants' that can lead to lifelong stress and unhealthy behaviours include stigmatised housing types, lack of control over one's day-to-day tasks at work, and the lack of respect acquired through a person's position in society.

The most radical and politically sensitive proposal to reduce health inequalities was set out in *The Spirit Level*, a treatise on the subject of inequality by the social epidemiologists Kate Pickett and Richard Wilkinson.[6] To put it simply, they believe that the focus for people who want to do something about health inequalities should be on reducing *socioeconomic* inequalities, both through redistribution via tax, and through employee-led control of salaries at the top and bottom of companies. This way, the social determinants of health are addressed 'upstream'.

On top of the solutions that come from business and government, there is a less-often discussed role that individuals can play. Those of us earning higher-than-average incomes often have positions in society that allow us to choose how we negotiate salaries, how we spend our money, and how we compare our consumption to everyone else around us. In the same way that the personal carbon footprint has led climate activists to adapt their lifestyles to sustainable levels, understanding one's share of the economic pie should lead inequality activists to adapt their lifestyles to comparably sustainable levels, in terms of relative income and wealth.

A further, more uncomfortable responsibility to consider is the mindset which the middle class has adopted towards the hierarchy in incomes, professions and educational achievement. As a generation, we value 'social mobility', often without respecting that there is nothing essentially wrong with individuals choosing to stay in lower-income jobs, or in opting out of further education. Perhaps alongside the promotion of socioeconomic equality, we should confront the stigmatisation of low status by respecting all social trajectories, whether stationary or mobile.

It is almost impossible to accurately predict the effect of such proposals on the level of health inequalities, or on the division of psychological wellbeing that these represent. Of course, obesity and smoking continue to be major causes of health inequalities. And, while these behaviours are to some extent mediated by stress, it is likely that there are some cultural and peer-related reasons why they may not be resolved simply through reducing stigmatisation or narrowing the gap between rich and poor. Still, as evidence continues to grow on the links between inequality, stigma, stress, behaviours, psychological wellbeing and health, it is time that we acted.

More money alone does not mean better health

If health inequalities need to be tackled outside of the health system, then what is the role of healthcare in this struggle? In a democracy, the greatest role a politician can play is ensuring access to healthcare by deciding how the system is financed. It is the politics of who pays, and how, that determines to what extent a health system addresses society's health problems.

When William Beveridge's idea of a publicly-funded National Health Service became a reality in 1947, health systems across most OECD countries followed suit. Their financing design ensured that the core objective remained equality of access for all. But, whilst public spending on healthcare has increased over time (averaging at around 7 per cent of GDP across OECD nations), relative spending has fallen in comparison with private expenditure. The US in particular, which has always opted for a market-based insurance system, has seen a rise in health expenditure from $1000 to $7,290 per person over the past twenty years – almost double that of the rest of the OECD countries.[7] What's worrying is that increased total spending has made little difference to the health status of populations, and, ironically, has as a result had a negative impact on overall health outcomes. In global terms, the diminishing return of life expectancy relative to increased spending, throws into question the effectiveness of healthcare services when the market takes control.[8] If more money isn't the answer to better health outcomes – then where are we going wrong?

The challenge presented itself during the 1980s, when ensuring a minimum level of access to resources came into conflict with reaching a certain level of 'efficiency'. Medical care costs increased so rapidly that spending rose from 3.8 per cent of GDP in 1960 to 7.2 per cent in 1980.[9] New medical devices, pills for all ills, and a market in healthcare – which became one of the world's most profitable industries – drove up the cost of state-provisioned care, which thus became unacceptably high. 'Cost-containment' – the capping of resources from the public pocket – became the watchword of the day; and redistribution through the market became the mechanism of choice.

The price of health

The encroaching market has created a culture where patients are being forced to act like consumers. This has long been the case in the US, where healthcare plans are sold to the highest bidder, medical treatment is advertised on television, and profit takes priority over clinical outcomes. But even in state-funded systems like the NHS, the consumer narrative is being played out in a way that serves to legitimise the scaling back of public investment in healthcare. We have seen this in the most recent health reforms, for example, where patients are even being actively encouraged to choose services their local GPs have not commissioned. What we see then is patients lining up to go to the shiny new PFI hospital that is spending large amounts of undisclosed tax-payer's money on

marketing, while the local town hospital falls out of popularity
having spent a lot less on marketing. The whole scenario leaves the
UK public wasting a lot of money, and there is very little we can do
to stop it.

If we are to maintain a sense of equality in our public services,
then continuing with the consumer approach is likely to cause more
harm than good. It is important to remember that healthcare is a
specific type of service – one that relies on trust between a patient
and a doctor. When money is being pooled into a system, the only
way an individual should influence how it is spent is through a
democratic process. The idea that patients are consumers is creating
a relationship between the health service and the public that is
increasingly individualistic. Encouraging this more individualistic
culture in patient care is causing both doctors and patients to walk
away from the NHS, to the detriment of the majority, and at the
expense of increasing health inequalities.

Our overriding aim should be to achieve equal access to good
quality healthcare, and make income irrelevant to the type of
healthcare one receives. Studies of health inequalities in developing
countries have shown that financing healthcare through taxation,
much in the way the NHS and other European countries' health
systems are funded, tends to be better for the poorest than the
alternatives.[10] But pooling money from progressive taxation does
more for a health system than just equitable redistribution; it
mandates government to keep records of health outcomes and use
of services; it develops competition for non-financial outcomes; and
it fosters greater participation in and ownership of public services
within the community.

Patients need to perceive of themselves as citizens – to feel an
intrinsic responsibility for their own health and the health of others.
By doing this they will not only value access to healthcare, but
health in itself. Regulation is undoubtedly needed to reign in
excessive healthcare costs, but spending will never reach the
'efficiencies' demanded by profit-based systems, especially with the

soaring disease burden of obesity, diabetes, heart disease and cancer. Our generation will have to accept the real cost of healthcare; the cost of providing every individual the right to care regardless of their ability to pay, their position in society and the illness they are suffering from.

Conclusions

Our first message is that a more equal society will produce a healthier population. This is because the health inequalities that we currently have are a reflection of the level of socioeconomic inequality that we tolerate – the divided lives and unequal experience of psychological wellbeing that we allow.

Our second message is that the decisions politicians make about our health system will not only influence our health, but will also affect our collective idea of our roles in society. An unequal and market-oriented healthcare system structure may change the way we value one another, and alter the attitudes we have towards our rights and responsibilities.

2011 saw the first instance of popular direct action taken in defence of the NHS. This was an encouraging development – even if it is worrying that such protest should be needed. But if our generation is truly concerned with the health and wellbeing of each individual in society, then we must do more than just defend the NHS. It is also essential that we fight against the forces that maintain and promote inequality in society, and which do so much to harm our nation's health.

Christo Albor grew up in the Philippines, but now lives in London. After finishing a degree in biology at Oxford in 2006, he taught sciences at a school in London for a year. In 2007 he began a PhD at York University, focusing on how socioeconomic inequalities within neighbourhoods across the UK affect health. In 2011 he started medical school, and now divides his time between studying and continuing to collaborate with researchers in ethnic and socioeconomic health inequalities across the UK, whilst attempting to broaden his research interests into medical fields.

Guppi Bola's medical and political interests came together when she was at Leeds University, where she committed most of her time to working with the global health group Medsin, co-founding the climate campaign Healthy Planet, as well as taking the first medical student delegation to the UNFCCC conference in Copenhagen. She is active in promoting the links between public health and social justice, focusing on climate change because of the obvious links between positive health and sustainability behaviours. After completing a masters in Global Health Science, she began work with the Essential Services campaigns team in Oxfam. She has most recently helped co-ordinate the anti-NHS reforms group @BigSocietyNHS and is now spending time learning how to tackle tax havens.

Notes

1. Dr Martin Luther King, Jr., address to the National Convention of the Medical Committee for Human Rights, Chicago, 25 March 1966.
2. R. Wilkinson, *Class and Health*, Tavistock Publications 1986.
3. There are many examples of these studies. Here are two which used a survey of civil servants (Whitehall Study): T. Chandola et al., 'Chronic stress at work and the metabolic syndrome: prospective study', *BMJ*, p.332, 2006; and H. Hemingway et al, 'Does autonomic function link social position to coronary risk? The Whitehall II study', *Circulation*, 111, 2005.
4. For example, see Davey Smith et al, 'Cortisol, testosterone, and coronary heart disease: prospective evidence from the Caerphilly study', *Circulation*, 112, 2005. For a study that links cortisol with socioeconomic status see M. Kristenson et al., 'Risk factors for coronary heart disease in different socioeconomic groups of Lithuania and Sweden – the LiVicordia Study', *Scand J Public Health*, 29, 2001. Also, for a general and enjoyable read on stress pathology see R. Sapolsky, *Why zebras don't get ulcers: an updated guide to stress, stress-related diseases, and coping*, Freeman and Company 1999.

5. M. Marmot, *Fair Society, Healthy Lives: The Marmot Review*, 2010.

6. R. Wilkinson & K. Pickett, *The Spirit Level: Why More Equal Societies Almost Always Do Better*, Allen Lane 2009.

7. D.A. Squires, 'The US Health System in Perspective; A Comparison of twelve industrialised nations', *Issues in International Health Policy*, Common Wealth Fund 2011.

8. Taken from UC Atlas of Global Inequality at http://ucatlas.ucsc.edu/spend.php

9. D.M. Cutler, 'Equality, Efficiency, and Market Fundamentals: The Dynamics of International Medical Care Reform', *Journal of Economic Literature*, 2002.

10. M. Makinen, H. Waters, M. Rauch, N. Almagambetova, R. Bitran, L. Gilson, D. McIntyre, S. Pannarunothai, A.L. Prieto, G. Ubilla, S. Ram, 'Inequalities in healthcare use and expenditures: empirical data from eight developing countries and countries in transition', *Bulletin of the World Health Organisation*, Geneva 2000.

All the news that's fit to sell: reforming the media for the next generation

Tim Holmes

One of the dominant political-cultural paradigms of the last few decades is what journalist Thomas Frank calls 'market populism'. As Frank describes it, this philosophy posits that, 'in addition to being mediums of exchange, markets are mediums of consent'. For market populists, 'the behaviour of markets is consistently understood as a transparent expression of the will of the people'. Markets 'give us what we want'. 'By their very nature', they 'confer democratic legitimacy'.[1]

This idea is especially obvious in dominant understandings of the mass media. Whatever faults they might have, papers and television channels are widely understood as reflecting the preferences of the public. As one article in *The Guardian* put it in 2007, 'the agenda of the national papers ... merely reflect[s] the tastes and wishes of their customers ... If you don't like what's in the papers, blame the readers, not the journalists'.[2]

This perception encourages, if not active approval, at least a shrug of the shoulders. While we may not like the media's content or activities, it suggests, they are nevertheless the outcome of a more or less democratic process. To change either – without arrogantly seeking to subvert this process of democratic representation – our efforts would best be directed at changing the prevailing culture our media simply articulates.

This is not the only argument generally offered in defence of the media (though it is probably the dominant one). We are told that, as organs of influence, the media are not up to much. As Nick Cohen puts it, 'the evidence that partisan newspapers and broadcasters do any more than preach to the converted is weak, to put it mildly'. We are told that the media facilitates a tolerable level of journalistic autonomy – again implying that interference will subvert another touchstone of democracy: a free press. In any case, like the cavalry, the internet has now come to the rescue, and 'the internet-connected citizen has too many sources of information for propagandists to control'.[3]

The reality can often be difficult to discern beneath the apologetics, so it is worth stating plainly. The mass media are vastly powerful agents, exerting a huge influence on both political decision making and public opinion.[4] They are dominated by centres of concentrated economic and political power. And their content and agenda largely reflect the influence of these dominant interests.

The media's power over political decision making is hardly disputed. As former Labour spin doctor Lance Price attests, '[n]o big decision could ever be made inside No. 10 without taking account of the likely reaction' of Rupert Murdoch – whose 'views counted for more than most actual cabinet ministers''. In the words of Lord Lipsey: 'as soon as you do something to upset a media company, they'll pour shit all over you'.[5]

The wishes of unelected proprietors and corporations matter precisely because owners exercise an extraordinary amount of power over the content their outlets put out. As Robert Maxwell noted shortly before his death, newspaper ownership 'gives me the power to raise issues effectively. In simple terms, it's a megaphone'. 'Proprietors set the political limits of the papers', writes former *Independent* editor Andrew Marr. As *The Sunday Times*' former editor Andrew Neil told Parliament:

> If you want to know what Rupert Murdoch really thinks then read the *Sun* and the *New York Post* ... the *Sun* reflects what Rupert thinks on every major issue.[6]

Some autonomy is passed to editors; but this hardly facilitates meaningful independence. 'Few modern editors fight their proprietors, because they will lose their jobs if they do', notes Marr: in general, 'the proprietor gets what he wants'. More fundamentally, proprietors appoint editors expected to be a safe pair of hands – people 'in general sympathy ideologically and philosophically', as former *Telegraph* owner Conrad Black put it. Neil concurs:

> Murdoch … picks the editors that will take the kind of view of these things that he has and these editors know what is expected of them when the big issues come and they fall into line.[7]

Since barriers to entry in media markets are considerable – only multimillionaires can overcome them – control accrues to extremely wealthy people. The natural result is a strong tilt to the right – Murdoch outlets' 'right-wing Republicanism … mixed with undiluted Thatcherism', or Black's 'instinctive sympathy for fellow multi-millionaires'. Even at the more 'liberal' end, Marr notes, 'rich men have rich men's politics' – and 'are not in the business to tax themselves harder or to help support political structures which will limit their reach'.[8]

Media companies are generally incorporated into larger conglomerates – and commercial considerations can limit the influence of owners. But they also *motivate* proprietorial pressure and interference – and the more commercial interests connected to a media company, the greater the potential for journalism to be corrupted or suppressed.

Ownership by profit-driven businesses has also perniciously driven the asset stripping of newsrooms. Outlets have always suffered resource constraints, adapting by covering predictable 'beats' and relying on external 'information subsidies', particularly powerful sources. In recent years, however, resources have been squeezed further, with fewer journalists given less time to produce much greater amounts of material. The internet has exacerbated this process, diverting advertising revenue and creating more space to fill. The result is that journalists are increasingly unable to leave their desks, check stories, or do much other than recycle agency copy and press releases. The space in which (resource-intensive) investigative journalism can be pursued is gradually being closed. In the meantime, the public relations industry has expanded vastly, leaving news media evermore vulnerable to manipulation.[9]

In general, journalists – paid employees selected partly for compliance – exercise little autonomy, let alone control. Thus, one seminal study concluded, 'News changes very little when the individuals that produce it are changed'. As veteran journalist Anthony Bevins has testified:

> It is daft to suggest that individuals can buck the system, ignore the pre-set 'taste' of their newspapers ... and survive. Dissident reporters who do not deliver the goods suffer professional death. They are ridden by news desks and backbench executives, they have their stories spiked on a systematic basis, they face the worst form of newspaper punishment – by-line deprivation ... It is much easier to pander to what the editors want.[10]

The result is an insidious process of self censorship. According to Isabel Hilton, '[y]ou stop functioning as a journalist. There are things you just don't bother to pursue because you know you just won't get them into the paper'. Professional norms of 'balance', 'impartiality' and 'objectivity' – generally applied not to protect the weak or uphold fairness but to placate powerful interests and reinforce the prevailing political elite consensus – provide little insulation.[11]

Popular pressure partly offsets these processes. But commercial media are not primarily responsive to the public. Their business model relies not on selling news to audiences but lucrative audiences to advertisers. Outlets depend on this revenue source because, notes the editor of one *Guardian* supplement:

No matter how many readers bought it, we would lose money, in
fact an increasing amount of money, without ad revenue –
unless we put the cover price up to what it really costs us to
make the paper, which is somewhere north of £5 a copy.[12]

Advertisers require a particular type of audience, 'buy[ing] space
through a complicated formula based' partly on 'the social profile of
the readership'. Moreover, 'it is now commonplace for news editors
to demand a particular story in order to appeal to some new target
group in the market place'.[13]

More fundamentally, popularity is simply not enough if an
outlet cannot attract audiences advertisers want. Historically this
has militated against papers of the left and the poor. Advertising
shortfalls forced highly popular downmarket left and liberal
papers the *Daily Sketch*, *News Chronicle* and *Daily Herald* to close
with circulations well over a million (roughly the *Telegraph*'s
circulation when the *Chronicle* closed). Yet the *Financial Times* has
long survived on a fraction of this circulation. Dependence on
advertisers has helped facilitate the political cleansing of the
British press.[14]

Advertisers may also influence content more directly, including
making content more amenable to commercial interests. Advertising
giant Procter & Gamble, for instance, instructs broadcasters that '[t]
here will be no material that will give offense, either directly or
indirectly to any commercial organisation of any sort', or 'which could
in any way further the concept of business as cold or ruthless'.[15]

Ownership by trusts can help mitigate the demands of
proprietor and profit, but little else. Likewise, public ownership and
funding can help circumvent some institutional constraints, but
only some – and bring problems of their own. In the UK, the
Government is able to appoint the BBC's senior staff and control its
funding, tending to both empower the Government and entrench
the prevailing political elite consensus at the heart of the
corporation. Moreover, the BBC is under continual attack from the

predators of the corporate sector, for whom it represents both unwelcome competition and an untapped market. State and corporate power have thus served continually to discipline and constrain the broadcaster throughout its history.

The consequences of this system have frequently been catastrophic. In the run up to the financial crisis, economic reporters blithely talked up the banks' toxic assets, even as the global economy was pushed closer to a cliff edge and a still-unfolding depression. In 2003 the media uncritically repeated state propaganda about Iraq's weapons of mass destruction designed to facilitate a war of aggression against a defenceless third world country. In the face of potentially catastrophic environmental threats, the story is much the same. On virtually every major issue, the existing media acts not as a servant of the public, but a propaganda organ of political and economic power.[16]

Notwithstanding the expansive claims made on its behalf, the internet appears to have changed little. A new medium alone can hardly make up for shortfalls in newsroom resources. Alternative online outlets populate the internet's 'back streets', not its 'main squares', and are read by a fraction of the population. For the relative few receiving most of their news online, mainstream outlets with established brands and substantial promotional resources still predominate: 'without promotion', one internet executive attests, 'you're just a lemonade stand on the highway'.[17] Meanwhile, a 'digital divide' still cuts off many of the poorer, older and less educated. There is even a serious threat of further enclosure of the digital commons, as rent-seeking cable and telephone companies lobby hard for the right (among others) to charge websites for speed of service. As US group Free Press note, the web would come to resemble cable TV.

The hope of something better is never assured. Nevertheless, the current crisis in mainstream journalism also presents opportunities. Newspapers are currently in a state of slow collapse: readership is declining, advertising revenue evaporating, and a public reluctant to pay for news offers little respite. The failure of profit-driven, corporate media is now impossible to overlook. 'Hackgate' presents just one example: in its quest to maximise profits, the popular press has transgressed the ethical and legal boundaries it has always avowed – its stranglehold over politics and law enforcement licensing a psychopathic, predatory role against innocent people. The self-regulatory PCC's role as an utterly complicit defender of the news industry (which state regulator Ofcom has astonishingly been encouraged to ape) has been comprehensively exposed.[18]

What comes next depends partly on what we are prepared to fight for. Ultimately, we must kick both profit motive and political elite out of mainstream media altogether. But there are important steps along the way. We must prevent corruption and facilitate diversity by restricting media ownership. The Leveson Inquiry might, if pushed, produce effective, independent media regulation. Public service requirements can be safeguarded and expanded. Government can incentivise non-profits and finance startup costs. Various models of state funding without state control offer varying degrees of public involvement: Scandinavia's model of neutrally-allocated funding (according to quantity of content and readership); tax rebates for non-profit media, allocated at citizens' behest; or allocating funds to investigative journalists directly through 'public commissioning' by citizens' councils.[19] These are all promising, and potentially complementary, models. But they can only be realised with concerted political pressure – from people like you and me.

Tim Holmes is a freelance writer, researcher and activist. His work has been published by *The Guardian*, New Left Project, Red Pepper, Znet, OpenDemocracy and elsewhere, and he has (co-)authored three reports for the Public Interest Research Centre. He lives in mid-Wales with his housemates and rats.

Notes

1. Thomas Frank, 'The Rise of Market Populism', *The Nation*, thenation. com/article/rise-market-populism?page=full, 30 October 2000.
2. Peter Wilby, 'Don't blame us – it's the readers' fault', *Guardian*, 17.12.07: guardian.co.uk/media/2007/dec/17/pressandpublishing.
3. Nick Cohen, 'Decline and fall of the puppetmasters', *Observer*, 17.7.11: guardian.co.uk/commentisfree/2011/jul17/nick-cohen-democracy-murdoch-mladic.
4. For a couple of good summaries, see James Curran, *Media and Power*, Routledge, 2002; Justin Lewis, *Constructing Public Opinion*, Columbia University Press, 2001.
5. Lance Price, 'Rupert Murdoch is effectively a member of Blair's cabinet', *The Guardian*, 1.7.06: www.guardian.co.uk/commentisfree/2006/jul/01/comment.rupertmurdoch;
Rupert Murdoch's influence in Britain', CBS News, 31.3.11: www.youtube.com/watch?v=Ua0OyucXvmc;
Maggie Brown, 'Who will be Ofcom's top dog?', *The Guardian*, 20.5.02: www.guardian.co.uk/media/2002/may/20/ofcom.mondaymediasection.
6. Brian McNair, *News and Journalism in the UK*, Routledge 1999, p53; Andrew Marr, *My Trade: A Short History of British Journalism*, Macmillan 2004; Andrew Neil, Minutes of evidence taken before the Select Committee on Communications: Media Ownership and the News, House of Lords, 23.1.08: www.publications.parliament.uk/pa/ld200708/ldselect/ldcomuni/122/8012302.htm.
7. Marr, op. cit., pp231, 235; James Curran and Jean Seaton, *Power Without Responsibility*, Routledge, 2003, p72; Neil, op. cit.
8. Andrew Neil, *Full Disclosure*, Pan Macmillan, 1997, p204; Max Hastings, *Editor: An Inside Story of Newspapers*, Pan Macmillan 2003, pp242-3; Marr, op. cit., p236.
9. See, for instance, Nick Davies, *Flat Earth News*, Chatto and Windus; Aeron Davis, *Public Relations Democracy: Public Relations, Politics and the Mass Media in Britain*, Manchester University Press 2002; Simon Cottle (ed.), *News, Public Relations and Power*, Sage 2003; Bob Franklin et al., 'The Quality and Independence of British Journalism', Cardiff University study, www.cardiff.ac.uk/jomec/resources/QualityIndependenceofBritishJournalism.pdf, 2006.
10. Curran and Seaton, op. cit., pp85, 336.
11. Ibid., p84.
12. 'Update: *The Guardian's* Spark Editor Responds', *Media Lens Media Alert*, 15.4.04: www.medialens.org/alerts/04/040415_Guardian_Spark_Response.HTM.

13. Marr, op cit., pp220-1; Nick Davies, 'Keeping a foot in the door', *The Guardian*, 10.1.00: www.guardian.co.uk/media/2000/jan/10/ mondaymediasection.pressandpublishing.

14. Curran and Seaton, op. cit.; Sharon Beder, *Global Spin: The Corporate Assault on Environmentalism*, Foxhole 2002.

15. Beder, op. cit., p192; Noreena Hertz, *The Silent Takeover: Global Capitalism and the Death of Democracy*, Arrow 2002, p7.

16. See, for instance, Dan Hind, *The Return of the Public*, Verso 2010; David Miller (ed.), *Tell Me Lies: Propaganda and Media Distortion in the Attack on Iraq*, Pluto Press 2004; Naomi Oreskes and Erik M. Conway, *Merchants of Doubt*, Bloomsbury 2010.

17. Curran and Seaton, op. cit., p270; James Curran, op. cit., p154.

18. See Natalie Fenton (ed.), *New Media, Old News*, Sage, pp65-6.

19. See, for instance, Dan Hind, op. cit.; Robert McChesney, *Communication Revolution*, New Press 2007; Curran, op cit.

Those yet to be born: representing the interests of future generations

Kirsty Schneeberger

Edmund Burke, the conservative philosopher, famously wrote of society as being 'a contract ... between those who are dead, those who are living, and those who are to be born'.[1] It may seem odd, in a book dedicated to radical politics for youth, to quote from the grandfather of modern conservatism. Moreover, the need to think for the long-term is not considered controversial even by present-day politicians. Nick Clegg, the Deputy Prime Minister, has spoken at length about the need for a 'horizon shift' in British politics to better represent long-term interests; and Ed Miliband, when Climate Change Secretary, frequently appealed to the rights of future generations – a theme he has continued as leader of the Opposition.[2]

Yet what is rhetorically fashionable remains very radical in practice. Very few of today's decision-makers have proven capable of translating their warm words into concrete action. In this regard, Burke's proposed social contract remains a radical one. For now, the agenda of the UK political system remains stuck on a trajectory where short-termism dominates the terms of debate and supersedes other approaches to governance.

Stealing from the future

At present we are stealing the future, selling it in the present, and calling it gross domestic product.

Paul Hawken[3]

The odds seem stacked against youth, not to mention future generations, and the old often become exasperated at the young for protesting so readily. Perhaps it is the nature of youth to find its voice and challenge the status quo as a rite of passage; but at least the young of each era have a voice, even if it is not always listened to by those in power. If a decision is made that will negatively impact on them they can demonstrate, write to their MP, vote in or out a particular government that aspires to represent their views. But where does that leave the silent constituency of the unborn – those future generations who will invariably be affected by decisions made today but who will have no say over their making?

The current political system does not include a mechanism for long-term accountability. At best it allows for a five-year perspective – and the impacts of decisions made by politicians voted in for that time will often reverberate for long after they have left office (and in some cases, long after they have died). This begs a profound question about how the British political system can move beyond the 'politics of now', to become more about the politics of the future. Radical? Not really. Necessary? Absolutely.

Realistic idealism

The latest earth systems science agrees that there are nine 'planetary boundaries' – ecological thresholds beyond which it would be dangerous for human civilisation to cross.[4] Of these we have already breached three (carbon dioxide levels in the atmosphere, biodiversity loss and the global nitrogen cycle); and we are likely to breach a fourth (the phosphorus cycle) in the near future.[5] Further recent work by Oxfam has considered the requirement for 'social floors' in conjunction with planetary boundaries, to bring equity into the discussion and ensure that a balance is struck in defining the ecological thresholds of the earth in a way that reflects the social dimensions of resource use and access.[6]

In defining a 'safe operating space' for humanity, the concept of planetary boundaries has established a firm platform from which to better understand the physical and ecological limits that we must stay within if we are to perpetuate life on earth as we know it.[7] This not only has serious implications for those alive today; it will significantly affect the lifestyles and environment of those born tomorrow.

The acceptance of planetary boundaries offers a potent framing for the environmental and social equity debate: one that may at first seem idealistic, but is in fact ruthlessly pragmatic. By setting the ground rules in which humanity's economic and political systems must operate, it shows up present-day assumptions about never-ending exponential growth and quarterly profit margins as dangerously short-termist fantasies. As Charlie Young and Rina Kuusipaolo explore elsewhere in this collection, we cannot go on increasing resource extraction to feed our consumer wants, and must differentiate these from our real needs, those that allow us to thrive and flourish – and will allow future generations to do the same.

The language around what is possible, what is realistic and what is sprinkled with wishful thinking is shifting. A large part of this is being catalysed by a growing awareness that decision-makers have a responsibility not only to the present day electorate, but also to posterity: that future generations do indeed have an interest in the governance of resources and natural capital as well as the economic system.[8] This interest ought then to be weighed up alongside the interests of present generations, and rightly so; but in a political system where these interests are considered equally, there would be greater likelihood of a decision that allows present generations to meet their needs without compromising the ability of future generations to meet theirs.[9]

An ombudsman for future generations

If future generations are to remember us more with gratitude than sorrow, we must achieve more than just the miracles of technology. We must also leave them a glimpse of the world as it was created, not just as it looked when we got through with it.

Lyndon B. Johnson, 1964[10]

If it is accepted that the interest of future generations ought to be factored into governance systems, then the mechanisms through which this can be achieved need to be explored.[11] In Hungary, there is a Parliamentary Commissioner for Future Generations, who receives petitions from the public to investigate whether or not a government decision will negatively impact on future generations, and then reports to Parliament.[12] Elsewhere, future generations have been granted legal standing to bring a case in the Philippines;[13] the International Court of Justice has heard arguments from states that refer to future generations;[14] and the Honourable Judge Weeramantry in the International Court of Justice has stated that the institution is very well placed to develop the body of law that is based on intergenerational equity.[15] In Canada, New Zealand and Israel, governments have established ministerial portfolios or parliamentary commissioners for future generations; in Finland, a Committee for the Future has been put in place. All have the aim of bringing long-term decision-making into the short-term political cycle.[16]

Of these forward-thinking examples, however, only the Hungarian one is in full operation; since 2008 its Commissioner has received over four hundred petitions from the public, and reported to the Hungarian Parliament after fully investigating approximately seventy of these.[17] The Office of the Commissioner focuses on environmental and sustainable development issues, and, by functioning as an ombudsman, effectively acts in a way that safeguards the Hungarian people's constitutional right to a clean and healthy environment. By extension, this is a right enjoyed by future generations, and so the Commissioner is able to take the long view by integrating the interests of posterity into his work.

Crucially, it is this right that underpins the very existence of the

Office, and it is the absence of such a right that has led some thinkers to argue that such a role could not exist in the UK owing to an absence of a similar constitutional right, or other right, that could be construed in a similar way.

Constitutional and environmental issues in the UK

It is true that the UK does not have such a right to a clean environment enshrined in its constitutional conventions – unlike many other countries both in Europe and across the world.[18] However, this does not necessarily preclude it from establishing an ombudsman or parliamentary commissioner with a wider portfolio.

Up until now, the foundation upon which proposals to institutionalise the rights of future generations has been built has been largely centred on environmental and sustainable development issues. Indeed, campaigns that are ongoing, or building on a new wave of momentum for the idea, tend to follow the line of extending environmental rights to future generations.[19] In many ways this makes perfect sense. At the very least, one generation owes it to the next and subsequent generations to give them the best chance of living fulfilled lives, and this is inextricably linked with the state of the environment.

Economic intergenerational injustices

However, the rights enjoyed by future generations do not end with environmental and sustainable development issues, important as they are. There are also intergenerational injustices that are currently being played out in relation to tax and other fiscal measures, housing, and pension policies.[20]

The ways in which policies on *all* matters are determined today do not adequately take into account the impacts they will have on tomorrow, and this has the potential to result in significant burdens being borne by future generations. In light of the growing understanding that intergenerational justice relates to more than environmental policies, it might be pertinent to consider how an ombudsman for future generations might have a role not only to act as a watchdog to protect the environmental needs of those people yet to be born, but also to investigate petitions from the public relating to other wider public policies.

In the absence of a constitutional right to a clean and healthy environment, the UK is perhaps better placed to establish an ombudsman with a broader remit than the Hungarian one: it might be feasible to instead focus on building on the rights to fair tax and pension policies, for instance, with environmental priorities a part of the ombudsman's broader portfolio.

In light of this, maybe we can begin to develop an appreciation for extending the existing rights to fair pensions, tax, housing, education and healthcare enjoyed by present generations to future generations. It would not be such a big step to consider that a right enjoyed by the population today should, in theory, be passed down to our descendants tomorrow.

In practice the situation is somewhat different, as research conducted into discount rates, the ways in which societies view young people and the iniquitous tax system bears out – so much so that it is questionable whether present-day decision-makers are really taking into account the impact that their policies will have on younger and future generations at all.[21]

It might be in vogue for politicians to use expressions like 'intergenerational equity' – for instance, when arguing – questionably – that cutting the deficit is being done to ensure that future generations are not burdened with financial debt; or to speak of the British promise, that one generation owes to the next to leave the world a better place. But actions really do speak louder than any rhetorical flourish, and it is clear that present policies are simply not delivering intergenerational justice across a broad spectrum of issues.

So perhaps it is time for an ombudsman, parliamentary

commissioner or even a Ministry for Future Generations, which could consider the impact of every political decision – not just those pertaining to the environment or sustainable development – and how these might impact on the young and those yet to be born.[22] In acting as a watchdog and mouthpiece for those who are not heard or cannot speak, such a figure could substantially contribute towards the safeguarding of our future for generations to come.

Kirsty Schneeberger joined Stakeholder Forum in 2011, having previously been the Coordinating Chair of the Department of Energy and Climate Change's youth Advisory Panel. Prior to that she was a coordinator of the UK Youth Climate Coalition, and since 2008 has participated in the UN climate negotiations advocating for intergenerational equity to be integrated into the process. Through this, she developed the campaign 'how old will you be in 2050?', which led to the online advocacy platform Think2050. She has also worked for WWF, CPRE and the Otesha Project and volunteered for various environmental charities. She is a Council Member of the UK Environmental Law Association, a trustee of the Public Interest Research Centre (PIRC), a Director of the ICE Coalition, and an adviser to the Intergenerational Foundation. In the 2010 she was awarded an MBE for her services to environmental conservation and her advocacy for young and future generations.

Notes

1. Edmund Burke, *Reflections on the Revolution in France*, 1790.
2. Nick Clegg, 'Horizon shift' speech, 9 September 2010: www.libdems.org. uk/news_detail.aspx?title=Nick_Clegg_speech:_Horizon_ shift&pPK=f8f7b543-d586-40e2-b4c9-e7be68970bf3;
   Ed Miliband, 'The Road to Copenhagen' speech, 19 November 2009: www2.lse.ac.uk/publicEvents/events/2009/20090826t1654z001.aspx;
   'Promise of Britain Speech' 23 May 2011:
   www.politics.co.uk/comment-analysis/2011/5/23/ed-miliband-promise-of-britain-speech-in-full.
3. Paul Hawken, Commencement Address to Class of 2009, 3.5.09,

University of Portland: http://www.paulhawken.com/paulhawken frameset.html.

4. See the Stockholm Resilience Centre (part of the Stockholm Environment Institute): www.stockholmresilience.org/planetary-boundaries.

5. Rockstrom et al., 'A safe operating space for humanity', *Nature*, 461, pp472-475, 24.9.09: www.nature.com/nature/journal/v461/n7263/full/461472a.html.

6. Kate Raworth, October 2011: *From planetary ceilings to social floors: can we live inside the doughnut?*: http://www.oxfamblogs.org/fp2p/?p=7237.

7. Rockstrom et al., op. cit.

8. The Rio +20 conference in 2012 dedicates one of the main themes to 'sustainable development governance', and as part of this there are promising proposals for the governance systems to bring the interests of future generations to the heart of the process. See for instance Dr Maja Göpel (*Ombudspersons for Future Generations as Sustainability Implementation Units*, SDG2012 October 2011): www.stakeholderforum.org/fileadmin/files/SDG%204%20Ombudspersons%20for%20Future%20Generations%20Thinkpiece.pdf

9. Brundtland Commission, *Our Common Future*, 1987.

10. From a speech Johnson gave after signing into law the Wilderness Act, 3 September 1964.

11. For a full analysis of the examples below and other institutional approaches to safeguarding the interests of future generations see K. Schneeberger, *Implementing intergenerational equity into mainstream decision-making*, 23 ELM, 2011: www.lawtext.com/pdfs/sampleArticles/ELMSCHNEEBERGER20to29.pdf

12. See the Parliamentary Commissioner's website: http://jno.hu/en/?&menu=home; for a full analysis of the role of each of the Commissioners see also P. Roderick *Taking the longer view*, 2010, p23: www.fdsd.org/wordpress/wp-content/uploads/Taking-the-longer-view-December-2010.pdf.

13. *Minors Oposa v Secretary of State for the Department of Environment and Natural Resources* [30 July 1993] 33 ILM 173(1994): www.jstor.org/pss/20693894.

14. *Pulp Mills*; Opinion of Cançado Trindade J (n7), p34.

15. *Nuclear Tests Case (New Zealand v France)* ICJ Reports 1995 Dissenting Opinion of Weeramantry J., p17.

16. For a full analysis of the role of each of these see P. Roderick, *Taking the longer view*, op. cit., p23.

17. Ibid.

18. See table 2, *Environmental Rights in European States' Constitutions*, in Roderick, op. cit., p19.

19. See the World Future Council campaign on this: www.futurejustice.org/

20. Matt Griffith, *Hoarding of Housing: the Intergenerational Crisis in the Housing Market*, Intergenerational Foundation, 19.10.11: http://www.if.org.uk/archives/1229/hoarding-of-housing-the-intergenerational-crisis-in-the-housing-market;
Maria Clara Murteira (2009), *The ethical relevance of inequalities in living standards between pensioners and their contemporaries*: http://soc.kuleuven.be/ceso/impalla/ESPANET/docs/Murteira_paper.pdf;
Angus Hanton, *Cashflow mentality exposes government short-termism*, Intergenerational Foundation, 23.8.11: www.if.org.uk/archives/988/cashflow-mentality-exposes-government-short-termism.

21. See Intergenerational Foundation website, www.if.org.uk/archives/832/the-light-taxation-of-wealthy-pensioners; and www.if.org.uk/archives/19/discount-rate.

22. The Alliance for Future Generations in the UK has already started working on this idea, and have published a mock website for just such a Ministry: www.ministryforfuturegenerations.org/.

Conclusion: Why should we care?

Deborah Grayson

> The ultimate market society is a childless society.
>
> Ulrich Beck[1]
>
> The end of history will be a very sad time.
>
> Francis Fukuyama[2]

During the party conferences in autumn 2011, journalist John Harris went out into the streets to find out if the mood amongst the general public matched the optimism of the leaders' speeches. Unsurprisingly, those he spoke to were considerably gloomier about the outlook than the country's elites – expressing concerns about jobs, cuts and another economic downturn. One woman told him that, given the insecurity she was facing, she had decided not to have children.[3]

While the economic crisis has doubtless contributed to unease about the prospect of starting a family, the trend of delaying marriage and parenthood, or rejecting them altogether, has been underway for the past four decades.[4] Of course, in that time there has been a huge cultural shift in terms of sexual mores and our expectations of relationships. There are many reasons why the nuclear family that was the norm for our grandparents' generation has become increasingly unpopular – not least the fact that it was predicated on the unpaid and unrecognised labour of women in the home. But for our generation these changes have gone beyond attempts to change the nature and structure of family life, into a more fundamental orientation away from families altogether. The common conflation of the two – marriage and kids – unhelpfully obscures this essential difference. A society without marriage could develop alternative legal and cultural institutions to preserve and validate relationships between adults; but while an individual life without children may be happy and fulfilled, a *society* without children would lose its stake in the future, and would suffer an intolerable crisis of meaning long before it literally died out.[5]

So, somebody must have children. Our reluctance to take on the responsibilities of parenthood has been dismissed by some as the desire for a prolonged adolescence, matching our atrophied attention spans and selfish depletion of our parents' wealth.[6] The more convincing explanation, outlined in this book and elsewhere, is that the demands of the neoliberal labour market, requiring us to be flexible, mobile, independent and capable of navigating uncertainty, are not easily compatible with having dependents.[7] The ultimate market society, as Beck says, is one without children, with no space for the essential acts of care that underpin our physical and mental well-being – and that make us capable of work. What is expected of us as adults within the economic sphere is fundamentally at odds with the committed familial relationships that still define social adulthood. It's little wonder that it is those who've given up on the idea of combining waged work with having a family – because they can live off one income, or because they'll subsist on minimal state support – who appear least conflicted about parenthood.

Neoliberalism cannot account for the existence of individuals outside of the workplace. This is not just children, the retired, or the long-term sick and disabled, but also otherwise healthy adults when they need to have time away from work to recover from illness, take holidays, care for relatives, or simply because the working day is over. These fundamental worker rights – to limit working hours and receive holiday and sick pay – have been viciously attacked as damaging to business, ignoring the fact that they were won in the first place because unhealthy, stressed and overburdened workforces are not as productive in the long term. The dynamics of shareholder capitalism, of course, mean there is little economic concern for long-term prospects, even for the businesses in which shareholders have invested.[8] But in human terms this situation is utterly unsustainable. The market conceives of us solely as individuals, but we are all dependent on other people for our health, well-being and ability to face the next working day. The current epidemic of mental health problems, which are now a bigger health burden in Europe than cancer and heart disease combined, is testament to what happens when we are forced to devalue our relationships in this way.[9]

Nor can neoliberalism account for the fact that when the work of social reproduction does become wage labour, it might have intrinsic values which are different from those in other sorts of work – which is why many of these jobs were placed in the public sector. As these jobs are outsourced to private companies, which employ transient, minimum-wage agency staff, these values are lost.[10] With few permanent positions and almost no opportunities for advancement, with little training or sense of purpose, those most likely to stay in these jobs are those who can detach from the boredom and frustration and perform their tasks in a perfunctory way: those who can 'not care'. Yet these companies also rely upon the fact that most workers *will* go beyond their contractual obligations – that the hospital porters who are forbidden from touching patients (for fear of litigation) won't just leave them in distress if they fall; that some basic and human quality will mean that the jobs get done even if they aren't being paid for. The horror stories of abuse in old people's homes and other institutions are actually surprisingly rare, considering the proportion of staff labouring under conditions in which any investment in the quality of the work being done is mercilessly exploited for profit.

This is the thing about care work: if you don't care it doesn't work. As such, our society is running on empty, undermining the most essential acts of social reproduction. The chapters in this book have provided dozens of examples of this unsustainable approach –

from Abdul Durant's plea for a living wage because his poverty
wages could barely clothe his family, to the prospect of inadequate
pensions pots which will condemn millions to near-destitution
upon retirement. They abound in every area – an education system
which focuses increasingly on 'market values', but has less and less
of a relationship with the jobs which are actually on offer; a health
service which uses the language of consumers and clients, breaking
down the trust and respect which is essential to the process of
getting better; an economic theory which can't even incorporate the
social limits of what humans need to be able to lead productive
lives, let alone the environmental limits of the physical world.

The sense of desperately seeking a human space which
recognises needs that cannot be bought or sold, and finding even
those spaces also colonised by the market's unsustainable focus on
the present, is exemplified, as Matthew Cheeseman argues, by the
night-time economy, where our need for friendship and solidarity is
bought at the price of our longer-term health and well-being. It's
not just that 10 million British adults are drinking at hazardous
levels, that the cost of alcohol harm is between £30 and £55 billion
a year, and that we are sitting on a time bomb of alcohol-related
cancers and liver damage.[11] It's that many people simply cannot
conceive of having a good time in another context, that there might
be life stages to come with other sorts of pleasures, that the future
might offer something other than a 'giant flag of surrender'. The
night-time economy's endless rehashing of the present perfectly
demonstrates the loss of a 'collective orientation towards the
future', as does a celebrity culture filled with faces like Demi Moore
and Brad Pitt, who seem hardly to have aged from idealised twenty-
something-hood since we were children.[12]

Solutions?

Fortunately, these chapters have also started to sketch out solutions.
The future will inevitably contain fewer natural resources, and what

we have come to identify as a desirable level of material consumption will need to be downgraded in the light of this. Accepting that we will be poorer, in today's terms, needs to be accompanied, as Noel Hatch says, with a renewed sense of our own power to shape the society that we want to live in. But it's arguable that fewer private material possessions doesn't necessarily have to lead to a marked drop in our standard of living, if we can reconfigure how we value the things we own in common. The examples of co-ownership given by Adam Ramsey and Ben Little show that we could have access to better housing and more secure energy, as well as more informed and engaged communities, if we can let go of our cultural obsession with sole ownership.

Several chapters emphasise the importance of intergenerational solidarity. Recognising our generation's particular role in challenging the status quo and building for the future cannot mean emphasising our own rights at the expense of other age groups, many of whom are highly vulnerable themselves. Doing so will not only allow those with power to pit us against our own parents, but will also see our generation fatally divided between those who go on to have children and those who do not. Similarly, the focus on unemployment and the need for meaningful work mustn't overemphasise the relationship between citizenship and labour. Yes, we have a right to work, but we also have a right to be cared for when we are in need, and a right to care for others in their turn. This reciprocity is an essential part of being human, and our working lives in the future must place at their heart the encouragement of this capacity. More equal pay, a 21-hour working week and a Citizens' Income, as well as a radical queer feminist politics which breaks down the gender binary and reasserts the caring capabilities of those in male bodies, could transform the relationship between work and the rest of our lives.[13]

The chapters in this book also suggest mechanisms for taking control of our future. We need, as George Gabriel says, to connect with the communities on our doorsteps, using the things we have in common – like the need for adequate pay – to build the solidarity that will help us understand our differences, opening up the possibility of mutual transformation. These bonds across age groups, unions, faiths and cultures will be essential if we are to take advantage of the forms of counterpower – such as strike action – which younger people are not well placed to exercise. The recent convergence of electricians on strike, Occupy London Stock Exchange, and student protesters on 9 November, shows that these connections are being made. Being willing to adapt our language and the focus of our targets in response to the changing political context will also be essential to our success. Richard George's advice is already being heeded on the ground: many of those involved in the student occupations last year, who responded to the appeal from Dale Farm to help resist eviction, and who are currently pitched up with the Occupy Movement, learned valuable skills from Climate Camp, and are taking their concern about climate change into new contexts without trying to make it the primary issue.

The buzzword of neoliberalism is 'choice' – the flipside of flexibilisation, which has masked the extreme lack of choice on offer in the political arena. The first step towards reclaiming our future has been to vocalise the fact that many of the things we've been offered as 'choices' – temporary work contracts, short-term leases – have felt more like a prison than freedom. Books such as *Lost Generation*, *Jilted Generation*, *Intern Nation* and *The Precariat*, along with the first book in this series, *Radical Future*, have been invaluable in charting the many ways in which the lives of young people today are poorer than those of our parents, despite our apparent wealth.[14] The second step is to begin to map out the *real* choices ahead of us, and to imagine a society fit to bring up children and grow old in. That's a conversation this book has attempted to begin. The 'very sad time' of Fukuyama's *End of History* is coming to a close. This book has shown that things can be different if we challenge the orthodoxies of the last thirty years with new ideas and ways of being. If we cohere as a generation and collaborate with all who share our hope for a better world, together we can make that future our reality.

Deborah Grayson has spent a lot of her time since 2008 in campaigning on climate change, democratic participation and electoral reform, and is starting work for the Coordinating Committee for Media Reform. As a writer she likes collaborations, working on a book about climate activism with Tamsin Omond, a paper about networks and nationalism with Ben Little, and a forthcoming book about drugs that will probably be annoying the *Daily Mail* this spring. She has now decided she wants to spend more time thinking, so she is doing a masters in Political Communications at Goldsmiths and hopes to carry on and do a PhD, if only to keep her Young Persons Railcard until she's 31. She lives on a boat on the Regents Canal and dreams of putting the world to rights so she can go back to plan A, being an opera director.

Notes

1. Ulrich Beck, *The Risk Society: Towards a New Modernity*, Sage 1992, p116.
2. Francis Fukuyama, *The End of History?*, The National Interest 1989.
3. John Harris, 'Breezy Optimism in the Political Bubble. Fear and Loathing on Britain's Streets', *Guardian* 2010: http://m.guardian.co.uk/commentisfree/2011/oct/05/conference-bubble-optimism-fear?cat=commentisfree&type=article.
4. Tomáš Sobotka, 'Shifting Parenthood to Advanced Reproductive Ages: Trends and Consequences', *Humanities, Social Sciences and Law* 201, 2, 2010.
5. This idea is famously explored in Baroness P. D. James's book *Children of Men*, Faber and Faber 1992.
6. Frank Furedi, *Children Who Won't Grow Up*, Spiked Online 2003.
7. Shiv Malik and Ed Howker, *Jilted Generation: How Britain has bankrupted its youth*, Icon Books 2010; Harry Blatterer, *Adulthood: the continuous redefinition of a social category*, Sociological Research Online 12(4)3 2007.
8. Ha-Joon Chang, *23 things they don't tell you about capitalism*, Allen Lane 2010.

9. A. Gustavsson et al., 'Cost of disorders of the brain in Europe 2010', *European Neuropsychopharmacology* 2011.

10. Polly Toynbee wrote about this from firsthand experience in her book *Hard Work: Life in Low-pay Britain*, Bloomsbury, 2003.

11. House of Commons Health Committee, *First Report – Alcohol*, 2010: www.publications.parliament.uk/pa/cm200910/cmselect/cmhealth/151/15102.htm.

12. Harry Blatterer, 'Adulthood: the continuous redefinition of a social category', *Sociological Research Online* 12(4)3 2007.

13. New Economics Foundation, *21 hours: why a shorter working week can help us all to flourish in the 21st century*, 2010: www.neweconomics.org/publications/21-hours; Green Party, *Citizens Income: an End to the Poverty Trap*: http://policy.greenparty.org.uk/policypointers/.

14. Patrick Ainley and Martin Allen, *Lost Generation? Strategies for Youth and Education*, Continuum 2010; Ross Perlin, *Intern Nation: how to earn nothing and learn little in the brave new economy*, Verso 2011; Guy Standing, *The Precariat: the new dangerous class*, Bloomsbury 2011; Ben Little (ed.), *Radical Future*, Soundings 2010.

Protest

Remember that time in *insert year*
when we marched through *insert town or city*
to march against *insert America*
after they invaded *insert country?*

You know that bright pink *insert article of clothing*
I wore and how *insert person* said *insert comment*
and we all said *insert reaction*. I'm sure
I've still got it somewhere in *insert location*

I suppose that's what it's like when you're *insert age*
and you're so completely sure that *insert worldview*.
You just think you can *insert expected outcome*, don't you?

David Floyd

This poem appears in the pamphlet *Protest* (Hearing Eye, 2011),
which is available from www.hearingeye.org, priced £4.